DONA RITA GUARAQUI, GUARDIAN OF THE CHURCH.

MAROBAVI:

A STUDY OF AN ASSIMILATED GROUP
IN NORTHERN SONORA

ROGER C. OWEN

NUMBER 3

ANTHROPOLOGICAL PAPERS

OF THE

UNIVERSITY OF ARIZONA

TUCSON

1959

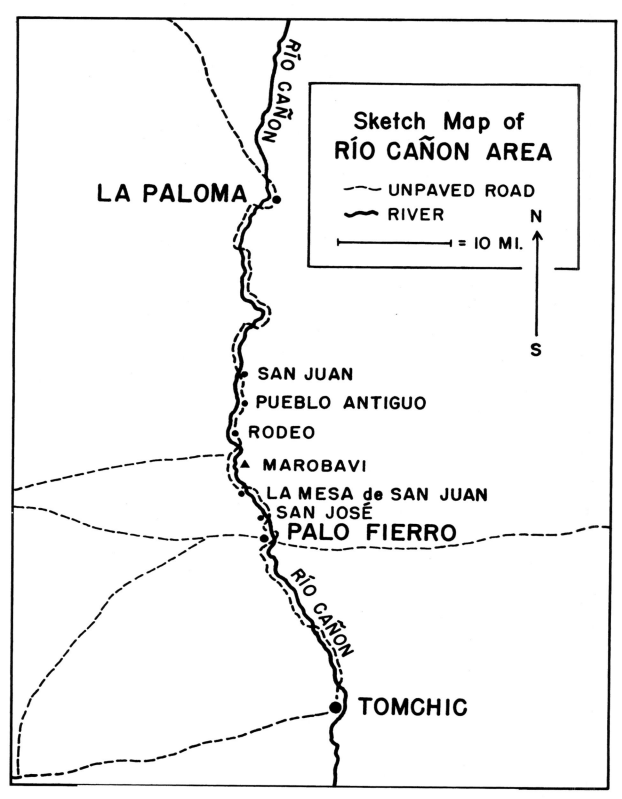

MAP 1. SKETCH MAP OF THE RIO CANON VALLEY REGION
OF NORTH-CENTRAL SONORA, MEXICO.

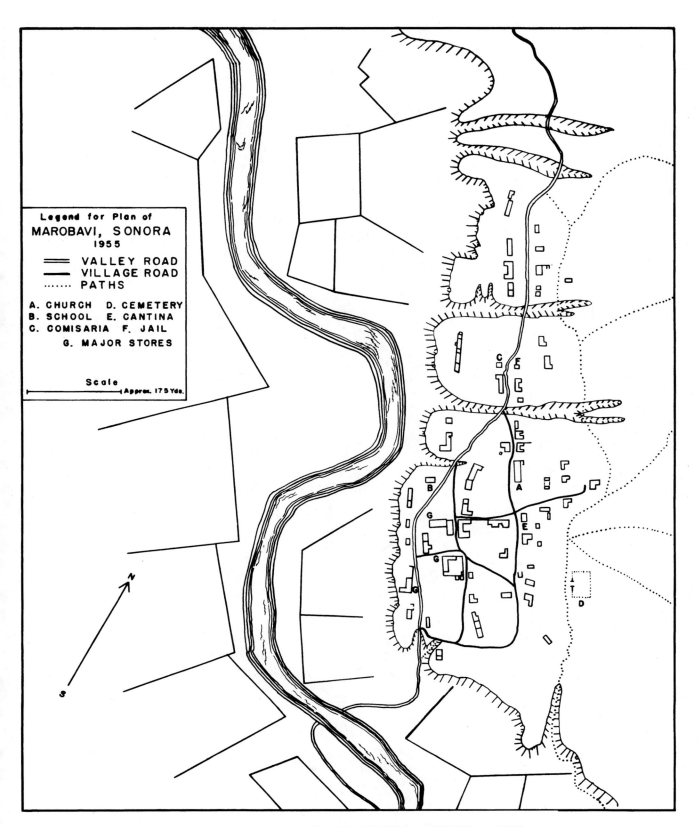

MAP 2. PLAN OF MAROBAVI, SONORA, MEXICO — 1955.

PREFACE

THIS REPORT attempts to describe certain aspects of life in a small village in north-central Sonora, Mexico. The data presented were collected over a five-month period — February to June, 1955 — during which time I spent seventy-one days in residence in Marobavi, which is a pseudonym.

Marobavi is located near what was, in aboriginal times, the western border of the Opata Indian area (Johnson 1950). The original impetus to this research was a curiosity regarding what, if anything, remained of the once complex culture of the Opata group. At the time this research project first was formulated very little knowledge was available regarding rural central Sonora, and it was then believed possible that some part of Opata culture might still survive. The Yaquis to the south demonstrated that such cultural survival was possible. Upon residence in the village it quickly became apparent that no such "survival" had occurred here. Then the research was focused on the social groups within the village with particular emphasis being placed on those people descendant from the aboriginal group.

In presenting this descriptive material, and in interpreting some of what I saw, I am aware that two months field research could have provided only incomplete, and possibly inaccurate data. If I had spent two years in the village I would have more confidence in the reliability of my observations and the validity of my conclusions. This report is considered by myself to be neither definitive nor complete, but is offered as an attempt to partially reduce the vacuum that exists in this area of Mexican ethnology.

Two very pertinent questions are not answered here: (1) What are the historical antecedents of the phenomena described and analyzed, and (2)

How "typical" an example is Marobavi of rural Sonoran society?[1] No attempt has been made herein to reconstruct Opata culture, nor to document the circumstances of Opata-Spanish, Opata-Mexican culture contact. I have studied the contemporary not just because of personal predilection but also due to the tremendous research time necessary to document the past to the point where reconstructed cultural and historical data may be used to interpret and explain contemporary behavior, if, indeed, that point can be reached. In regard to the representativeness of the village, again time in the field was a limiting factor. From the several visits made to nearby villages, and from frequent contact with their inhabitants, I believe that Marobavi is representative of some and, unquestionably, is not representative of others, even within the small valley where the village is located. Marobavi is in many ways isolated from the outside world. In the Río Cañon valley it is most similar to those towns and villages which are similarly isolated. The companion study by Hinton surveys the villages and towns of eastern Sonora.

While living in Marobavi I stayed in a small house rented from one of the villagers and ate with the family of the man from whom I was renting. When I first entered the valley I stressed an interest in the history of the region in general and its churches in particular. My initial reluctance to state explicitly my research interests was due to the reported sensitivity of the people in this section of Sonora to the term "Indian" and its application to themselves. Only during the first month or so of residence were questions frequent concerning my objectives in living in the village; later they were quite rare. I tried to explain exactly what I was studying to two individuals, but my objectives were not very clear even to them. Some people believed, until the last, that I was interested in mines or buried treasure, and others, at least at first, thought I was an undercover Protestant missionary.

The principal field techniques were observation, informal interviewing, and limited participation. I took a house-to-house census and all of the population figures used in this report, unless otherwise noted, are based on that.

Some of the roles I filled while in the village were portrait photographer, town common-transport, and host to many of the unoccupied men of the village, particularly during the evenings. Early in the field period men from the middle and lower status positions in Marobavi began frequenting my house. Usually there were from two to six men present each night and, at one time or another, all but two or three of the men of the village appeared. Other roles filled were hunting companion, baseball teammate, neighbor, boarder, English teacher, employer, customer, god-father to a *fariseo,* and many others. I knew all of the men of the village by sight and all but a few by name, and at various times talked with them all. With some of the women, however, few words were ever exchanged and only then because of the house-to-house census.

To varying degrees every household contributed data to the study. The bulk of the material comes from about twenty households. Among these are those headed by the civil and criminal judge, the judge of land use, several of the village's most active *mescal* makers, a *cantora* of the church, and the wealthiest man in the village. I had close personal relationships with the storekeeper who is the younger brother of the town's wealthiest man, one of the *cantoras,* the civil judge, and the large family with which I ate. Overt resistance to the study became evident only once when a young girl declined to answer the questions involved in the census. No reason for this was ever ascertained nor was the apparent breach ever healed. Relationships with the first man contacted in the village deteriorated badly late in the study but this did not appear to affect my status with other members of the village nor my close friendship with members of his family. With the rest of the people an easy pleasant acquaintanceship was established, and with some friendship.

A copy of the field notes on which this report is based is on file at the Department of Anthropology, University of Arizona, as is the small ethnological and archaeological collection made in conjunction with the study.

ACKNOWLEDGEMENTS

THIS REPORT was presented originally to the Department of Anthropology, University of Arizona, as a master's thesis. The research and writing were done under the direction and supervision of Dr. Edward H. Spicer. The field work was supported by a grant from the Ebin F. Comins Fund of the University of Arizona and I want to express my gratitude to the committee in charge of that fund for their vital aid.

I owe my introduction to Sonora and the Río Cañon valley to Thomas B. Hinton. His wide knowledge of Sonora, her people and history, and his comments and criticisms on this manuscript have been of special value to me. I should like to thank Jorge A. Martínez whose aid and advice through the years have helped me greatly in my attempt to understand Mexico.

Valuable comments, suggestions, and criticisms have been received from many people: Drs. Ralph Beals, Leonard Broom, Pedro Carrasco, Paul Ezell, William A. Lessa, the late George C. Barker, and others.

Without the aid of my wife, Suzanne M. Owen, this report would possibly be non-existant.

Finally, to the people of Marobavi, Sonora, who welcomed a curious and frequently inept stranger into their village, I want to say that those were seventy-one days enjoyably spent. I hope that they find my reporting neither inaccurate nor unpleasant.

ROGER C. OWEN

Ensenada, Baja California
July 1, 1959

CONTENTS

1

BACKGROUND

WHEN EUROPEANS first entered northern Sonora in 1536 it has been estimated that the population of the region may have exceeded 60,000 (Sauer 1935: 5). This figure, if correct, would include only those groups then identified as either Opatas or Jovas.[2] Authorities agree that the Opatas had a vigorous, well organized culture centering around irrigation agriculture. Further, they were pointed to as the cultural superiors of all the surrounding peoples. Europeans considered them " . . . the most highly civilized group between the northern limits of the Nahua area and the southwest or Pueblo region" (Bannon 1955: 13). Four hundred years later, after continuous European contact, it has been written that the Opatas " . . . have completely disappeared . . . as a cultural and ethnic entity" (Johnson 1950: 7). Though it is not the purpose here to explain the historical factors responsible for the destruction of Opata culture and society, the paragraphs which follow, outlining the history of the region, suggest some factors that must have been of basic importance.

Alvar Nuñez Cabeza de Vaca was thought to have been the first Spaniard to set foot in the Opata area. After wandering overland for several years from the eastern coast on the Gulf of Mexico, he passed through the Sonora River valley. This was in the year 1535 or 1536 (Smith 1929). The first Spaniard to lead a formal expedition to Sonora was Diego de Guzmán who led a military party north from Sinaloa to the Yaqui River in 1533. After making brief contact with the people there he turned back without having penetrated to the Opatería (Sauer 1932: 11-13). Following Guzmán was the Franciscan, Fray Marcos de Niza, who left Culiacán in 1539 to seek the fabled seven cities of gold, or Cíbola, that had been reported by de Vaca. Following up what may have been the Sonora River valley, de Niza was the first Spaniard deliberately to travel the entire length of what is now the state of Sonora. Later, in 1539, Melchior Díaz made a reconnaissance up the Sonora River, crossing over into the San Miguel valley to the west (Sauer 1932: 32-38).

The first settlement of Spaniards in central Sonora was established by Francisco Vasquez de Coronado in 1540. This settlement, called San Herónimo de los Corazones, was twice relocated and finally abandoned (Bannon 1955: 8). The next *entrada* into Sonora was not until 1565 when Francisco de Ibarra, having come north along the base of the Sierra Madre mountains, arrived in the vicinity of the village of Corazones. From here he went north and east, crossing over into what is now the state of Chihuahua. He eventually returned south, with his exit from the area marking the end of the period of pure exploration of the Sonoran region (Sauer 1932: 38-50).

Cabeza de Vaca was impressed by the generosity of the Indians around the village of Corazones (Smith 1929: 83), but it is reported that the ultimate result of the settlement planted by Coronado was the killing of forty of the settlers by these same Indians. Ibarra, who obtained news of the disaster from the Indians responsible, was favorably received by them (Hammond and Rey 1928: 162-163). For the most part the Opatas had only fleeting contacts with the traveling Spanish, and with few exceptions the relations between the two groups appear to have been friendly. Obregón reports that the destruction of the garrison at Corazones was due to the attentions paid the wives and daughters of the Indians by amorous Spanish soldiers. As a result of these liaisons the first two mestizo Sonorans were born.

Effective control of northern Sonora was achieved by missionaries, not by soldiers. The earliest records of mission activity in the Opata area begin in the second decade of the 17th century. The earliest known date for an Opata conversion is 1619 and apparently involved an Opata living among the Pima Bajo (Sauer 1935: 14). In 1622 two Jesuits, Padres Oliñano and Basilio, made a visit through the area of the Aivinos[3], preaching to the adults and baptizing four hundred children (Bannon 1955: 40-41). From this time on missionization and the introduction of Christianity proceeded rapidly. Records of baptisms commence in Santa María de Populo de Tónilce (Tónichi) in 1628 (Johnson 1950: 37). A mission was established at Sahuaripa in the same year, and another among the Batucos in 1629 (Bannon 1955: 45, 47). By 1660, little more than one hundred years after the Spanirds entered the Opata domain it was well covered by missions, and between 35,000 and 40,000 Indians had been baptized (Sauer 1935: 29).

Though the missionaries were often threatened with local revolt, only seldom did it occur, and throughout the period of mission establishment no major trouble with the Indians developed. Most of the now important towns in Sonora were founded during this period: Suaqui Grande in 1619; Onavas in 1622; Bacanora and Sahuaripa in 1629; Baviácora, Aconchi, Huépac, and Banámichi in 1639; Cucurpe, Opodepe, and Tuape in 1647-49; Magdalena, Oquitoa, and Caborca between 1689 and 1695, are a few (Villa 1951: 93).

In the wake of the missionaries came miners and land developers. For the next one hundred and fifty years, Sonora was the scene of constant turmoil as the clerics attempted to maintain their control over the Indians in the face of the newcomer's demands for laborers. The Jesuits, having formed villages of Indians around their missions, were under constant pressure to release their converts to work in mines and on ranches. In 1686 a royal *cédula* was sent to New Spain by Don Carlos II which prohibited the employment of new converts in either mines or on estates for a twenty year period after conversion. The practice of taking new converts for such work was cited as one reason for difficulty in introducing Christianity among the Pima Alto (Bolton 1948: 107-109). A later report by a Jesuit states that the Sonora Spaniards were of the "worst sort" and that by their bad example to the Indians who were lured to the mines, they greatly hindered the propagation of religion (Treutlein 1949: 241-242). This statement by Padre Pfefferkorn was written in 1794-95 of the period just before the expulsion of the Jesuits in 1767.

With the records of early missionization of the Opata region come reports of raids into the area by various nomadic groups. Records of these raids begin with the Suma in 1649 and 1651 (Sauer 1934: 70), and continue throughout the remainder of the 17th century. During this time the Janos, Jocomes and the Apaches all contributed to keeping the frontier unsettled (Bolton 1948: 162). During the latter part of the 17th century the Pimas and the Conchos, both sedentary agriculturalists, also fought the Spaniards in northern Sonora (Sauer 1934: 50, 70). The Pimas and the Apaches remained, but the Conchos were lost sight of by the early seventeen hundreds.

In the eighteenth century, Apache attacks increased in frequency and in the later 1700's were primarily responsible not only for keeping the frontier sections unsettled but also for wholesale population destruction and displacement as well. Their raids resulted in food shortages, widespread fear, and general chaos in the region, leading to drastic changes in the settlement patterns in northern Sonora. In the year 1762, of a former total of one hundred and ninety-eight inhabited places, only twenty-four remained, including towns, presidios, mines, farms, and ranches (Guitéras 1951: 144).

The problem presented by the Apache raids was further complicated by increasing hostility shown by the coastal dwelling Seri who, at this time, began to raid far inland. Apache and Seri attacks on the Spanish installations led one author, remarking epigrammatically on the state of health in Sonora, to say, "It's most deadly epidemic . . . has been for years, the arrow of the Seri and the spear of the Apache" (Guitéras 1951: 25). In 1751 Sonora's troubles were again increased with the revolt of the Pimas which, though put down the following year, resulted in the closing of most of the northern missions begun by Father Kino and his co-workers.

Difficulties with the Apaches reached a peak about 1850 (Wyllys 1932: 25), and then gradually abated as pressure was brought to bear on them in the north by the westward moving Americans. In the same period the Seri to the west were confined to their coastal strip by Mexican military action. Much of the area once abandoned was gradually reoccupied, though to this day many of the mines and ranches that were abandoned have never been reestablished. Legion are the stories of lost mines, buried mission treasure, and actual ruins of settlements, all dating from this period.

Sources covering the mission and colonial periods for northern Sonora are almost unanimous in citing several characteristics of the Opata-White contact situation. Among these are the following: (1) Mission fathers were sought and welcomed by the Indians, and Europeans in general found the Opatas willing and cooperative workers; (2) European material culture, religion, and language were eagerly adopted by the Indians; (3) Cultural transmission was fostered by frequent intermarriage and the formation of other enduring social relationships entered into by the Indians and the Spanish; (4) The Opatas were first-class soldiers who, though only rarely turning these talents against the Europeans, were in almost continuous conflict with the Apaches.

The only large scale Opata rebellion took place in 1821 and was neither long lasting nor widespread (Hardy 1829: 55). The Opatas did take part in the various disturbances in Sonora following the Mexican war of Independence; an Opata, second in command to the Yaqui Banderas, was taken to Arispe and shot in 1832 (Nye 1861: 55). About this time Opatas were employed as regular soldiers to staff the various

presidios along the northern frontier and also as foot soldiers to pursue raiding Apaches. There was a company of Opata soldiers stationed at Ures around 1850 which was used to fight the raiders (Bartlett 1854: 444), and a report from another traveler cites the presence of soldiers in Chihuahua City in 1806 who were " . . . of a nation called Opejas (sic), and are said to be the best soldiers in New Spain . . . they appear to be fine, stout, athletic men, and were the most subordinate and faithful troops I ever knew, acting as a band of brothers . . . " (Coues 1895: 773).

During the 19th century extensive de-tribalization took place among the Opatas. At this time the various local or regional ethnic designations used in the earlier sources (Aibines, Batucos, Sonoras, Hehues, Tehuimas, Eudeves, etc.) gave way to the generic term "Opata" and as time progressed even this name was supplanted by the general term *indio* or Indian. Since the early part of the 17th century the Indians had been moved first from their small *rancherías* to mission settlements, from the mission settlements to mines and *haciendas,* and from all of these they were frequently displaced by the various hostile Indian groups. Beginning with the work of the Jesuit missionaries, and continuing with the ministrations of civil officials, mine owners, *hacendados,* and army officers, the Opatas were continually exposed to Europeans and European culture. By the end of the 19th century there was no whole identifiable as Opata culture, and Opata society had been reduced from a group of well integrated, smoothly functioning sub-tribes, to groups of individuals who practiced Spanish cultural patterns for the most part, and who were to some degree incorporated within Mexican rural society. This point is well made in a report describing the situation in the Bavispe valley in the year 1890:

> This territory was once the possession of the large tribe of Opata Indians, who are now civilized. They have lost their language, religion, and traditions, dress like the Mexicans, and in appearance are in no way distinguishable from the laboring class of Mexico with which they are merged through frequent intermarriages (Lumholtz 1912: 10).

Another report describes the same condition prevailing in the western part of the Opatería in 1902 and further cites the Indians' reluctance to speak their own language or to behave in any way that would distinguish them from their neighbors Hrdlicka 1904: 57).

Today, in the Río Cañon valley, this reluctance to identify with an aboriginal group is still found among those who may admit Indian ancestry. It is recognized as a fact by the inhabitants of the valley that some of their co-residents are descended from the *indígenas* or *antepasados*[4], and it is also recognized that some are not. Yet few of either group, the Indian descendant or the White descendant, know with any degree of certainty who the aboriginal inhabitants of the valley were culturally, or what they were called. During the period of this study a continuous attempt was made to elicit from informants a name to apply to the Indians of the region. In the early part of the study the most common term received was "Aztec" from Indians and Whites alike, and both at times mentioned Pima and Yaqui as possibilities. Only a few informants

mentioned Opata, and the people who did were predominantly those considered in the village as being non-Indian. Only one person showed complete assurance in answering Opata; many of the villagers freely stated that they did not know, and many others appeared to guess. Later in the study more people admitted Opata ancestry, but in no case did anyone claim ties with a contemporary ethnic group bearing that name.

In 1902 it was said of the Indians of the Río Cañon valley, "The tribe is disappearing in a manner exceptional among American tribes—by voluntary amalgamation with the white . . . " (Hrdlicka 1904: 71). It is clear that the tribe has indeed disappeared and that the still present descendants of people who were members of the tribe are now part of the general population. The following chapters examine one small village in an attempt to describe the result of "voluntary amalgamation" by: (1) describing the contemporary culture of Marobavi; (2) analyzing the social segments within the village, and; (3) by examining Indian-White cultural and social relations in the light of present acculturation theory.

2

THE VILLAGE OF MAROBAVI

LOCATION

THE VALLEY of the Río Cañon is one of several major river valleys in north-central and north-eastern Sonora. Bordered on both east and west by low mountain ranges, the river valley runs from north to south for a distance of fifty miles before it joins that of another river, turns to the west, and runs to the Gulf of California.

Distances from one valley to the next are not great, but the only roads are single lane, unpaved and ungraded, and east-west travel is difficult at any time of the year. During the wet summer months all of the roads may be closed for days or even a week or more, due to either mud or land slides. Most of the travel out of the Río Cañon valley is to the west; there is very little contact with the towns in the valley to the east. No public transportation enters the valley of the Río Cañon and even the best of the roads provide a nearly impossible path for a standard automobile. There is, however, a steady flow of privately owned trucks to and from the towns in the valley to the west; all commercial supplies for the valley come in in this manner.

North-south travel in the river valley is by means of a dirt road that frequently runs directly up the water course. Except after rains the river rarely has more than a foot or so of water in it, and its sandy bottom provides a safe, smooth road bed for those accustomed to it. For the stranger driving without a guide travel on this road may seem to consist of a semi-continuous progression from one patch of mud to the next, interrupted only by pauses to allow the ignition to dry. The road connects all of the settlements in the valley to each other and both its northern and southern ends connect with the major road in the valley to the west.

There are five towns in the Río Cañon valley that range in size from nearly 2000 people to less than 100; Marobavi has 312 (see Map 1). La Paloma, the northernmost town in the valley, has about 400 inhabitants. It was founded sometime around 1650 as a Jesuit mission to the Eudeve Indians (Villa 1951: 93; Bolton 1948, Vol. 1: 51), and the ruins of the old mission may still be seen. La Paloma is the seat of a *municipio* which includes ranches and settlements to the north and west, and though intimately linked historically with the southern part of the Cañon valley, it now has many more ties with the towns to the west than with the villages to the south. From La Paloma the road runs through a narrow, red-rock canyon for fifteen miles before the valley widens slightly and the next town is reached. San Juan, like La Paloma, was founded in the 17th century as a Jesuit mission. For the last fifty years it has been declining in population; it has few more than one hundred people at present.

Between La Paloma and San Juan the narrow valley contains several small settlements, mostly single-family ranches located at the mouths of small arroyos. To this point there is usually a flow of water above ground but, to the south where the valley widens out, most of the flow is underground except during the rainy period in the summer.

Five miles south of San Juan is Pueblo Antiguo, a village of about 150 people. Unlike the two towns to the north, neither church nor store are found here, hence it is strongly dependent on Marobavi for supplies and the services of the church. Five miles to the south Marobavi is located on an alluvial terrace overlooking the valley which, at this point, is one-half mile wide. From Marobavi the road continues south past two small settlements and after crossing the river a dozen or more times reaches Palo Fierro. This town is the second largest in the valley and is the seat of the *municipio* which includes San Juan, Pueblo Antiguo, Marobavi and a small town in the valley to the west. It is fifteen miles south of Marobavi and nearly forty miles from La Paloma. Depending on the driver's knowledge of the road the trip may take from two to eight hours or more.

From Palo Fierro roads lead in all directions and it is the only point in the Río Cañon valley from which the valley to the east may be reached by truck. Below Palo Fierro is Tomchic, a growing town with a present population of nearly 2000 people. It is connected to Palo Fierro by eighteen miles of good road which is heavily traveled by trucks; much of the commerce in the valley is carried over this route. At Tomchic the valley road climbs up and over the mountains, and then descends in the valley to the west.

In the Río Cañon valley, small one and two-family ranches are located between all the towns and villages, and the observer is impressed by the number of habitations and the amount of agricultural activity. Only a few stretches of the river valley are untouched; all of the land suitable for farming is cultivated at some time of the year and hence fenced off from the cattle that browse along the river course. In addition to the ubiquitous cattle, men on horseback and women and children afoot are often encountered along the river bed.

DESCRIPTION OF THE VILLAGE

THE TERRACE on which Marobavi is built lies on the east side of the valley and is raised about fifty feet above the flood plain of the river. At this point the river is dry for all but the rainy months. Entering the town from the south, the road cuts across the river bed and climbs up to the village through a rocky trough cut through the terrace face. The road returns to level land in front of a small store and across from a large area free of houses but overgrown with brush. The village, not laid out in the conventional Mex-

ican style with a central plaza and blocks of houses, is composed of houses placed singly and in groups, spread out over a distance of half a mile on both sides of the road (see Map 2). All the stores, the school, the church, and most of the larger houses are located at the southern end of the village. Here also are two plaza-like areas, though neither is more than a vacant area clear of weeds. From the edge of the terrace a view may be had of the valley winding to the north and to the south, with the agricultural land that pertains to the village spread out below on both sides of the river course. Across the valley from the village, behind the alluvial plain, terraces and ridges lead up to the higher hills beyond, while to the rear of the village brush-covered ridges rise rapidly, ultimately reaching the higher hills and mountains of the Sierra de San Marcos.

Though not as old as Palo Fierro, San Juan, or La Paloma, Marobavi has been a recognized settlement since sometime before 1763 when it was mentioned as an abandoned ranch, depopulated as a result of Apache depredations in the area (Guitéras 1951: 143). It was reinhabited sometime before 1828 when it was cited as one of the populated places in the Río Cañon valley (Hardy 1829: map). Census reports for the year 1895 indicate that it was inhabited then (Resúmenes 1895: 48), and this was verified by the town's older people. It has been continuously inhabited since the 1880's and it seems highly probable, from informants' statements, that the village has continued to be inhabited since the early 19th century. From time to time stone projectile points, three-quarter grooved axes, stone mortars and pestles, and pieces of other stone artifacts turn up, indicating a possible pre-European contact habitation of the terrace top. Most of these artifacts when found, excluding the projectile points, are put to use by the contemporary villagers.[5]

The village contains seventy-eight structures all made of adobe brick or some combination of adobe brick, brush, and rocks. Only one house in the village has a complete exterior surface of plaster or stucco. Most of the houses, due to the effect of the weather on the unprotected, exposed brick surfaces, appear extremely old and worn even when comparatively new and structurally sound. Roofs commonly are made of successive layers of cane and brush, mud, more brush, and finally, more dirt. This type of roof sheds water until it reaches the point of saturation, then it begins to leak continuously, often after the rain has stopped. Two buildings in the village have tin roofs, one being the largest store and the other the home with the stuccoed exterior walls. No window glass exists in the village, and none of the houses has effective screening; most have none at all. In all but two houses the floors consist of hard packed dirt. These two exceptions have cement flooring in some of the rooms.

There are two house-types in the village. One is a flat-roofed, adobe brick structure where the walls provide support for the roof beams. This house-type is found throughout Mexico and, with some variation, particularly in size, has formed the principal style of architecture in much of rural northern Mexico. The other house-type, called locally the *casa de dos naves* or the house of two naves[6], is an adaptation of the framework used in wattle-and-daub construction to the use of adobe bricks for walls. The bricks are fitted between, or sometimes around, the notched corner posts, and these posts provide support for the system of beams upon which the roof is built. Down the center, on the long axis, runs a large beam, called the *madre viga,* which is supported by two notched poles slightly higher than any of the corner posts, and this beam in turn supports the smaller stringers that hold up the roof. The roof, which is slightly peaked, is made of the same materials used in the other house-type. Frequently so much brush and dirt is applied that the house appears to be flat-roofed from the outside. These houses, usually excavated slightly (12 to 18 inches) on the inside, present a low silhouette, particularly when contrasted with the square, high ceilinged, flat-roofed adobe houses. Many do not have chimneys or smoke holes, and some have no windows. By using two or more frames of these *casas de dos naves,* houses of two or more rooms may be built, but most of those in Marobavi consist of only

one room and an attached cooking ramada. Where the cooking ramada is present, the adobe structure is used solely as a sleeping room.

The villagers say that two houses here are of an older type. These, *casas de dos naves* in framework, have walls made of mortared stream cobbles instead of walls of adobe brick. Many of the house ruins, particularly those found around the church, appear to be from houses of this type. When this type of house was built the women constructed the walls; that is, they did the mortaring. Now only men engage in house construction, and rocks are used only as a footing for adobe bricks.

In the flat-roofed house style the interior walls are often plastered and whitewashed but in the *casa de dos naves* almost never. The interiors of most houses are dark, many rooms being illuminated only by the light coming in at the door. Windows, few in number in all of the houses, are always provided with closeable shutters and often barred with iron grills. In even the best houses household furnishings are sparse and at most include plain wooden chairs and tables, simple cabinets, and beds in a few. In the poorest homes furniture is almost non-existent —an old chair or two, a wobbly home-made table, a sitting bench made of a split log with pegged legs added, and a few wooden or cardboard boxes holding a few possessions. In the *casa de dos naves* most of these items are found in the cooking ramada. The sleeping room contains only a few holy pictures on the walls, a calendar, possibly an old trunk, and in the corner, out of the way, the rolled up sleeping mats made of plaited palm fronds. These mats, or *petates,* are used for sleeping by well over half of the villagers.

In the *casas de dos naves* and in most of the poorer houses the ramada is the family and social center, and it is here that guests are received. When used in such a way the ramada is often walled on all sides, but when associated with the adobe houses where the kitchen is inside, ramadas are most often simple sunshades attached to the rear of the house. Only two or three houses in the village have sitting rooms, not devoted to sleeping or eating. The kitchen is the customary place to entertain guests.

Cooking is done over a wood fire built in a clay fire-box. When outdoors, the box is built upon a clay platform about two and one-half feet high and consists of a solid platform with a fire area on top enclosed on three sides by clay walls about ten inches high and about two inches thick. When indoors, these fire boxes may be placed in the corner with a metal or clay flue drawing off the smoke or, as in many houses, they are located in one wall of the kitchen. In the latter case the wall devoted to the fire-box is double, and a space of two to four feet separates the interior wall from the exterior. This open space, with the fire-box placed in the middle, serves as a chimney and as a storage space for utensils.

Most cooking utensils are of blue enameled metalware, with the infrequently made clay ollas used to contain water. Various sizes of tin cans, in addition to the clay pottery, are used for water and for storage. Clay fire plates, or *comales,* are not used; instead a flattened piece of tin or steel serves as a base on which to rest pots over the fire. Other kitchen furnishings include metal grinders used for meats, coffee, and corn, *metates,* either the tripod type bought at the store or slab type found in the bush, both one and two-handed uniface manos, galvanized water buckets used to bring in water from the wells, and in some of the homes, cannister sets, cupboards, and wooden shelves used to store miscellaneous items. Glass jars and bottles are highly prized because of their impermeability to insects, animals, and dampness, and also because of their scarcity.

None of the houses has electricity or running water. The only source of electric power in the village is a gasoline-powered generator. This machine is privately owned and is used to provide light in the village *cantina,* and to provide illumination for outdoor dances. All water used in the homes is transported by hand either from wells located in back of many of the houses or from the irrigation ditches that run at the base of the terrace face. No homes have interior plumbing and only three have exterior privies. Elimination takes place in the arroyos and bushy patches in and around the village. When houses have ramadas used for animals, set off from the living unit, women use these for the necessities.

There are four public buildings in the village; the church, the school, the *comisaría,* and the jail. The church is the largest single structure in the community and is now in disrepair (see Chapter 5). The school building is a small, one room adobe structure undistinguished in any way except by the flagpole which stands in front. The *comisaría,* or the office of the local *municipio* official, is smaller still, and is used to conduct formal civil matters and as a repository for local records. The jail, made notable by the large iron-barred door hanging loose on its hinges, is only about seven feet square, and is rarely used. There are no two-storied buildings in the village, but there is marked contrast in silhouette between the square flat-roofed adobes and the lower *casas de dos naves.* Many of the latter type hardly exceed six feet in height, contrasting with ten to fifteen for the other.

THE PEOPLE

THERE are fifty-nine households in Marobavi, a household herein being considered as those people who sleep under the same roof, and who share cooking facilities with this group alone. Forty households occupy separate houses set off from other nearby units by open space, brush, and trees, plus distances that range from a few feet to fifty yards or more. Nineteen families reside in eight multiple dwellings with each of the families occupying a complete apartment.

Houses are built on parcels of land of irregular size and the land associated with any house may stretch to the rear, to the front, or surround the house on all sides. Such land is as often unfenced as fenced. Some units have corrals near the house where cattle, horses, and mules are kept but outbuildings are rare and where they do exist they are small brush huts used for pigs and chickens. Many houses located on the eroding terrace face have no land attached to them other than that upon which they are built.

The sex and age distributions of the village's 312 people are shown in Table 1[7]. They are nearly identical to those of rural Mexico as a whole

(Whetten 1948: 65-71). The figures include only those people who are said to be "of Marobavi," those people who live on the terrace itself or on nearby ranches which are traditionally considered to be socially connected to the village. There are three ranches in this category. Their inhabitants are members of families the major part of which live in Marobavi. The children from these ranches are to be seen in the village daily, the men from them often working in the village.

There is some question regarding the size of Marobavi in the recent past. Many of the villagers disagree on this point. Some say that at the turn of the century the site was virtually abandoned; others state that it was about the same size then as now. Census figures for 1895 show the population of Marobavi as 269 (Resúmenes 1895: 48), and others, six years later, have it at 245 (Censo 1901). In trying to estimate the size of the earlier population, the number of house ruins, which is great, is of little help. When a house is no longer structurally sound it is abandoned, the usable beams salvaged, and then used in the new house, usually located nearby. To repair a *casa de dos naves* it is necessary to virtually rebuild it by replanting the structural posts or replacing them, clearing away the accumulated debris, and constructing a new roof. It is easier to move to a new location and start afresh. One old man could point to the ruins of two houses near the one in which he now lives wherein, during his seventy-eight years, he had resided.

The physical types found within the village are extremely varied. There are blondes with blue eyes and fair skin, red-heads, people with extremely dark skin, hair and eyes, and people who show these characteristics in various combinations. Many families display constellations of physical characteristics that strongly suggest American Indian ancestors: extremely dark hair, skin and eyes, marked lip eversion, moderate to well-developed epicanthic fold, flaring nostrils combined with a short, low nose bridge, scant facial hair, short stature, and others. Contrasting with this group are many people who display none of these characteristics and who, physically, would be indistinguishable from a northern Euro-

pean-derived population. In addition to these distinctly different physical types there are many individuals who have, to varying degrees, some features associated with both groups. For the purposes of this paper these three physical types will be considered as three points on a continuum of phenotype; Indian, Mestizo, and White. It should be made explicitly clear, however, that these terms are not meant to delineate racial-historical background. Instead the terms, which will be clearly defined in the following chapters, are used here as they are used by the residents of Marobavi and are social as well as racial categories.

LANGUAGE AND EDUCATION

THE ONLY LANGUAGE spoken in Marobavi is Spanish. The aboriginal language is entirely gone and is remembered in the speech of the present inhabitants by only a few place names, names of plants, and a word or two in the general vocabulary. Throughout the period of this study an attempt was made to find a speaker of Opata and, though continual reports were had of this or that old person who remembered the language, no individual was ever found who knew more than a few words of a language referred to as Opata. Some of the Whites in Marobavi felt that some of the older Indians should be able to speak it, but as each was approached the ability was denied. Many stated that their parents spoke the language but they themselves were not taught it.

Many of the men in the village have passed periods of time in the United States, but the only person who has a command of English is a store-keeper who has learned it from books alone. Many of the men know words and phrases but only the storekeeper can converse. They attribute their inability to speak English to the fact that they associated primarily with Mexicans while in the United States. The only other language represented in the village is Yaqui; some of the men who have worked in the southern part of the state learned a few words.

Formal education is received in a one room school building facing the "plaza." The building is plain on the outside, and unadorned on the inside except for a blackboard hanging at the front of the room. There are seats and benches for about thirty-five pupils but places to write for about half that number. The school offers only the first three grades and specializes in reading, writing, arithmetic, and Mexican history. World geography and general history are also taught. Many students attend not only the initial three years, but also the major part of the eligible age period, which is from six to fifteen years of age. These children, usually girls, repeat the various offerings several times. Though attendance is nominally compulsory, many children attend only sporadically and others not at all. On any given day during school, groups of children may be seen playing in the streets, and even among those whose interest is high attendance often suffers due to illness, agricultural work, or family affairs.

The school in Marobavi is run by the federal government and all funds for its operation come from Mexico City. Two daily sessions are held, one in the morning and one in the afternoon, and each takes about two hours. The school draws pupils from both Rodeo and La Mesa, neither of which has its own. In these three communities and in the nearby ranches there are ninety children of the proper age to attend school; only forty-seven are enrolled at the present time and rarely more than thirty attend on any single day. The total figure of eligible-age children, ninety, includes an unknown number who may have finished three or more years of classes, so the discrepancies between possible and actual number of enrollees is not as great as it seems. Those students wishing more education must leave the *municipio* as none of the schools in it goes higher than the 6th grade. The school teacher, who is very well paid by Marobavi standards, receives six hundred pesos a month. She herself has a sixth grade education in schools very similar to that of Marobavi.

The illiteracy rate for the town is not known. Many of the adult men have difficulty reading and some cannot write, many of them from the more well-to-do families. There has been a school in Marobavi since at least 1893 when the annual treasury report contains an item covering school expenses in the village (Cuenta 1894). The present school building was constructed sometime within the last ten years.

THE LARGER COMMUNITY

TO MOST of the village dwellers the *municipio* is the largest unit of personal interaction; it encompasses the area in which, in the normal course of the year's events, they may expect to travel. Most of the people of Marobavi will visit Palo Fierro at least once a year and some go once a week or even more frequently, particularly men. Men often go to "el pueblo" for no other reason than for a change of scenery or to visit friends; when women go, there is usually some social event, a wedding, a funeral, a baseball game. Several of the older and poorer women of Marobavi have not been to Palo Fierro for several years, while the town's more mobile residents, the truck owners, make weekly or bi-weekly trips to towns in the valley to the west and less often to Hermosillo, Nogales, and even Tucson. As braceros or *alambristas,* as the "wet-backs" are known locally, many of the town's males have covered most of Sonora, the southwestern United States, the American west coast states, and some have been as far east as Chicago.

There is much contact between the inhabitants of Marobavi and the two nearby settlements of La Mesa and Rodeo. Many of the people living in these three places are related, and almost all have strong economic and social ties. The children of the two nearby settlements come to Marobavi to school and many of them pass the day there. Adults come to the store or to work, dances and parties in any of the three towns are attended by people from the other two. Church services in Marobavi are attended by people from both Rodeo and La Mesa, and many of the inhabitants of both places come to Marobavi to pass their leisure time.

Contact with Palo Fierro, Pueblo Antiguo, and San Juan is more casual, and though most or all of the inhabitants of these several villages know each other by name, the Marobavian views the residents of these more distant villages with some suspicion. The remark was often passed that some caution was necessary when passing through San Juan, that the people there were liable to cause trouble. No dangerous individuals were ever named; the feeling is directed toward the inhabitants generally. A similar unexplained feeling is present in the village directed against other Marobavians. An emphasis is placed on keeping doors and windows closed and locked when the house is unguarded, to keep out both animals and "bad people." A determined burglar would have no difficulty in entering the most secured house since the customary method is to pull the door closed from the outside while at the same time pulling a chair up against the inside of the closing door. No tales of past thefts from houses were ever heard, nor were attempts to uncover the name of one "bad person" successful. This feeling of suspicion is intensified the further one moves, figuratively, from the village. While strong feelings of identification are felt by all Marobavians with the state of Sonora, the Marobavian is not quite sure that all others in the state are as law abiding as himself; in fact, he is sure they are not. Attachment to Mexico as a nation, though strong, is less personal than the feeling toward the state. With the nation they identify themselves against other nations; with Sonora they unite against the rest of Mexico. This attitude toward the Mexican State would be readily understandable to an American "state's righter"; the Republic has meaning principally as it is composed of people from Sonora. The derogatory term *"guacho"* (Sp. *guache:* tough, despicable man) is applied to all Mexicans not born in Sonora, particularly if they are from the southern states (Foster 1948: 33). This dislike of southern Mexicans may stem from the lack of contact with them, almost none of the inhabitants of Marobavi ever having been in any other Mexican state.

Such names as Tucson, Bisbee, Phoenix, and Los Angeles are more familiar to the villagers than are the names of Mexico's major cities. All of the people have had at least second-hand accounts of these American cities and a great many of the men have been in one or more of them. No one from the village has ever been to Mexico City or Guad-

alajara, and very few have ever been in Sinaloa, the next state to the south. Attitudes toward the United States in general are favorable. Most of the braceros have had good experiences while working in the north, or at least they have had enough pleasant times to balance the unpleasant. Some men remarked on harsh bosses or border officials, and there were many tales of hardships encountered, particularly when the individual had been a "wet-back," yet most seemed to consider the trips as adventures to be savored and long remembered. A trip to the United States is considered a valuable part of a youth's training for manhood. There he will see something of the world, make some money, learn new agricultural techniques, and then return to his home a man more firmly convinced of the benefits to be had in his own village. It does not always work this way. An unknown number of migrants have not returned, and there are a few men in the village who, coming back every few years, remain in Marobavi a few months only to leave again. Reasons given by those who, having been to the United States, returned and remained in their own village, stress the negative aspects of life in the United States rather than the positive aspects of life in Marobavi, e.g. "the work is too hard and steady," "the hours are too long," "it costs too much to live," or life is just "too different."[8]

From outside, the valley appears to be extremely isolated, connected to the rest of the world by only a few dirt roads; a truck, several hours, and some determination are required to traverse from the highway to the valley road. There is no public transportation that travels this route, and all travel into the region must either be by personal vehicle or arranged in advance with one of the commercial truckers. From inside the valley looking out, the world does not seem far off. Continuous contact is maintained through travelers who, by truck or horse, pass through the villages almost daily. These people carry news from one village to the next, and often from one valley to another. Traveling salesmen, cattle buyers, and cowboys all stop in each town either at the store or at a house, have a drink, and talk.

There is no telephone or telegraph service into this section of the valley, though there is to both Tomchic and La Paloma. There are two battery-operated radios in the village, and when these are turned on, they are usually tuned to music. One newspaper finds its way into Marobavi regularly; this is a Catholic weekly printed in Hermosillo that contains news of church affairs in northern Sonora. In addition, some magazines are found in the homes, though none is subscribed to regularly. Within the town are several Spiegel catalogues, all a few years old, that are used as guides in making clothing, as well as for general reading material. A few books are also found in some of the homes and are, primarily, either religious texts or school primers.

People are fairly up-to-date concerning happenings in Palo Fierro and the other nearby valley towns. They know who has sold what land, who is getting married to whom, what the price of corn is, when the next dance will be held, what religious observances are being held, what important personages have visited the valley, and other matters of local importance. Official dicta are rapidly transmitted among the villages of the *municipio* either by means of the weekly mail service, by travelers, or by means of special messengers. News of happenings in other valleys and in the state capital may take a week or more to reach Marobavi. In the spring of 1955 several men were interested in obtaining contracts to go to the United States to work as agricultural laborers, and ultimately the only way they could obtain accurate information on this subject of vital interest was to make the trip to Hermosillo itself, less than one hundred miles away.

Of Mexico as a whole they have little recent information, and of the world at large the best informed are from six months to a year behind. For most of the villagers such knowledge has little meaning, and their lack of knowledge concerning world events is as much due to a lack of interest as to any scarcity of accurate information. Prevalent topics of conversation within the village are current happenings in the town— the crops and cattle, neighbors, children, social events — rather than those events which are happening or will happen in the outside world.

3

MAKING A LIVING

THE BASIS of community subsistence in Marobavi is the earth, as it is throughout the Río
Cañon valley and most of northern Sonora as
well. The livelihood of the Marobavian depends
on his ability to extract his living from the none-
too-hospitable land. Only one family in the village does not rely on direct contact with the physical environment for the majority of its income.
Livelihood is derived from three major sources;
farming and cattle raising, wage work, and the
manufacture of the alcoholic beverage, *mescal*.

FARMING AND CATTLE RAISING

THE Río Cañon river, as it passes the town, is
a winding, gravelly, sandy bed. Dry for most of
the year, it flows only during the summer and
after rains in the winter. After a heavy summer
rain the river becomes a torrent, rushing over the
low banks and spreading out onto the surrounding
low land, and often it becomes several hundred
feet wide. It is this flood plain which serves the
agricultural needs of the villagers. The deposits of
alluvium here cover an area about three fourths
of a mile in width, stretching from the base of
the terrace-face upon which the village is built
to the alluvial fans coming down from the hills
on the other side of the valley.[9] No crops of
importance are cultivated anywhere but on the
flood plain; none is raised in the desert around
the village, and only flowers and a few fruit trees
are to be found within the village itself.

The main crops raised are wheat, corn, beans,
and cotton. Less important ones include onions,
chili peppers, garlic, tobacco, watermelons, can-
taloupes, and a small amount of citrus fruits.
The first group listed includes all of the items
planted to large plots of land; the second group
includes those crops usually sown to small patches
on the edge of the major plantings. Formerly sugar
cane was of importance in this area as was
tobacco, and large quantities of the dark sugar
called *panocha* were made and exported (Hewes
1935). Wheat was introduced here by the early
Jesuit missionaries and is now the crop to which
the greatest acreage is devoted. Wheat is planted
in the late fall, in October or November, and is
harvested in May or June. The land on which
it is planted is often double cropped, with either
corn or beans or both being sown after the wheat
is harvested. Cotton was first grown in Marobavi
in 1953 though it has been raised in the Tomchic
and La Paloma areas for some years. Cotton has
a long growing season as contrasted with wheat
or corn, and the growing periods of the latter two
overlap with that of cotton. If cotton is to be successful in the valley, the villagers believe, it must
be planted in March or early in April. Thus if
cotton is to be planted in a field, it may not be
used for wheat. Cotton is first picked some time
in September, and the picking continues on into
the fall, so a field planted to cotton is not only
denied to wheat but to corn and beans as well.
At this time there is a controversy in the village
regarding what is to be planted. More than half
of the cultivators in Marobavi are now sowing
cotton instead of food plants. Of the estimated
three hundred acres of land that belong to people
of the village, about half are in cotton, a quarter
planted to either beans or corn, and the rest
lying fallow after having yielded winter wheat.

Though some agriculture is attempted without
irrigation, often the difference between harvesting
a crop and turning in the animals to graze over
a dried up field lies in the availability of supplementary water.

The villagers say the river is drying up, that
formerly, due to much heavier rains, the river

flowed more strongly and more regularly. A possible testimony to a former greater abundance of water is given by the old irrigation ditches lining the banks of the stream and built into the terrace-faces; they now fail to capture the river water that runs from one to three feet below their entrances. The only surface water that can be led onto the fields of Marobavi is that given by a small spring that bubbles up just below the cliff at the south end of the village. Even this water may be used for land holdings only at some distance from the village due to the necessity for the *milpas* to be of a lower altitude than the spring. To alleviate the water shortage, and also to reduce the uncertainty of the yield, mechanized irrigation has been introduced. Wells utilizing pumps have been used for a number of years in the Río Cañon valley but the first one was introduced into this village about 1950, another added a year or so later, and a third is now complete. These wells are located to the north of the settlement, and, by using a system of simple dirt ditches, are in a position to pump water to almost all of the agricultural land of the community. All of the wells and pumps are privately owned by two men of the town who use them primarily to irrigate their own land. Any excess water is sold to other cultivators for either cash or a share of the crops.

Agricultural technology practiced in the area is representative of the modern and complex as well as the simple and traditional. Technology is in a state of transition. A tractor, various types of planting machines, a thresher, and caterpillar tractors are locally owned. All of these machines are owned by the same men who own the wells, and are used by those who, in some way, manage to "rent" them from the well-owners. Mechanized agriculture contrasts strongly with that based on the mule-drawn plows, spades, and hand labor practiced by the majority of the cultivators. The villagers escape from the limitations of hand cultivation to the extent that they are successful in making an arrangement with the machine owners.

The threshing machine was first used in the village in 1954, and proved unsatisfactory. It broke down during the harvest and, as replacement parts were not immediately available, much of the still unthreshed wheat was ruined when a hail storm arrived. In 1955 all of the farmers, not trusting the machine, went back to the old method. To thresh the wheat the grain-bearing heads are all piled in a circular enclosure and horses and mules are driven around over the piled up grain. Neither the animals nor the men like this technique; the horses become dizzy and nervous from continuous circling, and the men are plagued by small, sharp barbs given off by the grain. This system has apparently persisted almost unchanged, in form and in the attitudes of the participants, since mission times (Treutlein 1949: 47-48).

Until recently most of the wheat was ground on double-stoned grinding mills motivated by burro power. These mills are small, with the stones about three feet across. When used, women were responsible for producing flour from the grain brought in from the fields by the men. Now almost all of the grain is taken to Palo Fierro to be ground in the modern mill. Some stone mills, which are occasionally used, may still be found in Marobavi.

The most common agricultural tools are the spade and the hoe, both serving a variety of uses, and, combined with the plow they provide the only tools used by the poorer cultivators. These tools are used until completely worn out, then repaired and re-used. New heads for the spade and the hoe are fashioned by the village blacksmith, and new handles are carved by several individuals. Some tools have been repaired so often that no part of the original metal or wood remains. There is a strong awareness in the village of modern agricultural methods and machines, obtained by the men who have been in the United States. Yet all but the rich and those associated with them in agriculture are denied any but the traditional due to the cost of machines, wells, fertilizers, etc. To clear any new land, for example, it is necessary to use a caterpillar tractor on the heavy, dense growth that covers the uncultivated river bottom. The nearest bulldozer is located at Tomchic, and to bring it to Marobavi it is necessary to pay rent from the time it leaves Tomchic until it returns. The rental rate for machine and driver is seventy pesos per hour, and nearly two days are needed to bring it from Tomchic alone. New land, highly desirable with the advent of the mechanized wells, is denied to most of the agriculturalists of Marobavi.

Landholdings in the village have been small in the past, and for most villagers they still are. A man who has twenty *hectarias* (2.47 acres per *hectaria),* is thought to be well-to-do; use or ownership of less than two or three *hectarias* is not uncommon. There still remains an estimated one hundred *hectarias* of uncultivated land in the river bottom near the village overgrown with scrub growth. Much of this land is heavily covered with sand and gravel due to floods, and hence is at best only marginally usable, and some of it is former arable land that has had its potential destroyed by river action. With the exception of one village resident who is clearing land below La Mesa de San Juan where river water is available for irrigation, all of the land now being cleared is controlled by a few wealthy individuals.

This points to the two types of agriculture practiced in the village as well as to the differential participation in agriculture, in both the proprietary and technological senses, of the different village households. Speculation plays some part in all agricultural activities in Marobavi due to the practice in the community of selling a large part of the harvest for cash and then later repurchasing the staples as they are needed. Most of the households aim at subsistence, hoping to produce enough to provide food and cash to last out the year. Only corn is stored by many families, and even this may be sold if the need for cash arises. Contrasting with this subsistence-oriented behavior on the part of most of the villagers are three households that engage in agriculture for profit and the amassing of wealth. These families are headed by the owners of the two major stores, and the married son of one of the two. It is these men who own the wells and the pumps that can now give water to the dry lands. In the past they have planted wheat, corn, and beans on their own land and then sold water to others at the rate of one hundred pesos for twelve hours of irrigation. Along with the outright sale of water they have farmed *medias,* or shares, with other individ-

uals. The well-owner provides water, some help at harvest time, and possibly the seed; the other provides the land, the bulk of the labor, and that part of the seed which he is able. The actual arrangements vary depending on the wealth position of the land owner and, on the basis of who provides what, some split is made in the eventual crop. The well-owner usually receives fifty per cent or more of the produce as his share. With the introduction of cotton last year the *media* system reached fruition.

Wheat, corn, and beans do not require the amount of water, imported seed, insecticides, and harvesting labor as does cotton. On the other hand, none of these crops has the per acre cash yield of the purely cash crop. In order to plant cotton, twenty households entered into partnerships with the well-owners.

Of the fifty-nine households in Marobavi only twenty-five state that they are land owners. Of these twenty-five, three are known to have mortgaged their land and are not able to use it, another has land located several miles below the village and does not participate in the economy of Marobavi, while three more households are not using their land either because of poor land conditions or because of a lack of free water. This leaves eighteen families in the community farming on land owned by themselves and this figure includes the three rich households. Deducting these three from the total of independent land-owning farmers, fifteen remain, and of these fifteen six are share farmers with one or another of the well-owners. At this time then, there are only nine households that own land and are engaged in agriculture as free agents. Only five of these are possessors of enough land to allow them more than a minimal subsistence income and, interestingly, four of these five have land below the village where the waters derived from the spring and from the reemerging river may be used for irrigation. The amount of land actually owned by the three wealthy households is not known, but judging from estimates by the villagers, the figure of eighty *hectarias* would not be far wrong. One of the three has around fifty, and the father-son team splits the remainder.

Associated with farming and generally engaged in by the same households is cattle raising. Only one household receives its income exclusively from the sale of cattle, and some twenty-eight households own small numbers of animals ranging from a single animal to as high as one hundred. Only four of these families own less than three head, and five own more than fifty. The other twenty families range between these two figures, tending toward the small numbers—five to ten. The cattle are a mixture of white-faced Herefords and the older "range" steer type. An occasional animal shows signs, with the spread of its horns, of its "long-horn" ancestry. Cattle are allowed to roam at will in the desert and in the river itself. At all times large numbers of animals are to be found browsing on the greenery that grows along the river bank, walking in the water, and frequently disputing the right of way with travelers. Only at calving time are many cows herded into the village, and even then many are left to have their offspring where they will. There is a high mortality rate in calves. Owners hear of the location of their cattle, all of which are branded, from travelers, hunters, and others traversing the river or desert, while less welcome news is transmitted by a flock of circling buzzards.

Animals are killed usually for some fiesta or social occasion, wedding, saint's day fiestas, or visits from esteemed friends. During the period of this study a cow was butchered in the village about every two weeks and fresh meat was not available between times.

To the non-expert eye the cattle appear thin and wild and the meat they yield is tough and stringy. No attempt is made to fatten the animal before killing. The animal is butchered by felling it with an axe, and then cutting its throat. It is then skinned and gutted on the spot, and the meat filleted from the bones. In hot weather the meat is consumed or otherwise disposed of the day of the butchering. In colder weather the fresh meat may be kept for two or three days. The owner of the animal distributes various chunks of meat to those people who help him, often other members of his kin group, keeps what he himself will require, and then vends the remainder

to those villagers wishing to buy it. Some meat is always dried by placing it in the sun, off the ground and out of reach of all non-flying creatures.

Cattle raising, like agriculture, is dependent for success on the availability of water. When the river dries up completely, or when there is insufficient rainfall to replenish the browse, many cattle are lost. There is little grass cover on the hills surrounding the village so the animals browse over brush and cacti as well as the greenery found along the river. A slight disturbance in the spring and summer rainfall pattern is enough to upset the balance between sufficient forage and starvation. In the hot summer months of 1954 around seventy head of cattle out of an estimated total of four hundred were lost.

While some animals are killed to be eaten, most are sold for cash to traveling cattle buyers or to other villagers. There is an awareness that the range will carry only a limited number of animals, so the herd is thinned out continuously at both the top and the bottom. Calves and young animals are sold, older ones eaten. Cattle values range from a couple of hundred pesos to six or seven hundred depending on age and size. A strong young steer brings four or five hundred, a calf only two hundred and fifty, while a large, well built cow or steer is valued at as much as seven hundred pesos.

Horses, though not playing an important part in the exchange economy of the village, are extremely important as the primary means of male transportation. Boys learn to ride at an early age and it is not uncommon to see a child of three or four astride a horse being held in place by an older child or an adult sitting behind. Horses have a high value and a good one is worth as much as a thousand pesos or more. A few families have a mule or two used primarily to pull the plow. Burros abound in the village, and are used for light hauling and for human transportation. They are ridden mostly by children. Mules are valued at around two hundred and fifty pesos and burros at the extremely low price of twenty to thirty pesos—less than the price of a good pair of shoes. Burros appear to need little or no attention to aid them in rather rapid multiplication.

Some of the excess animals in the village are sold to ranches that specialize in butchering burros and drying their meat. This dry meat is then sold over northern Sonora as *carne seca,* or dried meat, usually assumed to be beef. No one in Marobavi raises horses, mules, or burros directly for profit; any one family raises and keeps the number of animals that they may expect to use. Some profit is realized from that part of the natural increase which is not needed, the surplus animals being either sold or traded.

Other domestic animals include chickens, dogs, pigs, turkeys, cats, and goats in the order of approximate frequency. Almost all households have some chickens and a dog or two, the former providing eggs and the latter only companionship. Pigs are kept by less than half of the household and a sow with shoats has a high value, often bringing as much as three hundred pesos. Cats are kept as pets, and turkeys for their meat. Only one man has a herd of goats and he sells most of their meat outside of the village.

MESCAL

MESCAL, a tequila-like beverage, is made from the distilled juice of the roasted and fermented head of a small agave plant. These plants are collected in the hills where they grow wild, the long pointed leaves cut off, and the round cabbage-like remainder is put into an earth oven to be roasted. The oven is a stone-lined, bell-shaped excavation about six feet deep, with the narrow part of the bell at the top where the small entrance is located. Before the heads are inserted, a large wood fire is built in the oven and allowed to burn for a day or so until the rock lining of the oven is red hot. The *mescal* heads are then inserted, the oven closed, and cooking proceeds for about four days. After the oven has cooled, the cooked heads are removed and are now ready for fermentation. All of the cooked plants are richly brown and contain a quantity of thick, sweet syrup. In eating *mescal,* the individual leaf stalks are stripped from the head and chewed to extract the juice, and the wad of coarse fiber that remains in the mouth is spat out. When numbers of these fiber wads are seen around the village it is a good sign that a new batch of the beverage has been brought in. Cooked *mescal,* though very popular with the children, does not play an important part in the diet of the villagers.

The next step in making the drink is to place the cooked, sugary heads in smaller stone-lined pits where fermentation will take place. These pits, about four feet long, two wide, and three feet deep, are located a few yards from the earth oven, and in them, after being splashed with a "starter" (fermented juice left from the last run), the cooked heads are covered over with burlap and allowed to remain for another four days. Following this period the now fermented heads are taken from the pits and removed to the still for distillation. The still is made of two 50 gallon drums, one for cooking, the other for condensing the vapor. They are connected to each other by a piece of makeshift pipe. A fire is built under the drum in which the heads have been placed along with a small quantity of water. The resultant steam is led off into the other drum by means of the connecting pipe, and there, due to the water contained by the second drum, the steam condenses. The liquid so produced, still in the pipe, is led out of the side of the water drum and slowly drips into a five gallon tin. The only control exerted over the nature of the beverage is the taste of the operator; if he thinks it too weak, he redistills the run. The process ends when the operator feels that the liquid is of sufficient potency, and the liquid still draining from the end of the tube no longer has *mescal* content.

A total of about fifteen days is required to produce a run of the drink, with about eight of these days spent in actual work. Four or five days are necessary to collect the heads, another couple to cut the wood, heat the oven, and insert the heads, another to transfer them to the fermentation pits, and about two for distilling. Two men usually cooperate in the production of *mescal,* both sharing in the work and the proceeds. From an average run between five and ten gallons are produced and each gallon brings thirty pesos, an average return to each of the two men of something less than ten pesos per day for the fifteen day period.

There are three active stills in Marobavi that, in total, produce about fifteen gallons a month during the dry season. _Mescal_ is not made during the summer rainy months because of the effect ground water has on the earth ovens. Two of these stills are owned by one man who does not make the beverage himself; for the use of his equipment, he charges the _mescaleros_ one litre out of every five gallons made. Making _mescal_ in Marobavi is a bootleg operation and violates the Mexican tax laws. In the past there have been raids on the stills of the village by federal or state agents, but in recent years the _mescaleros_ have not been bothered. This may be due to the fact that at this time little or none of the local produce is sold outside of the village, whereas in the past it was trucked out in some quantity.

The method of distribution of _mescal_ within the village is particularly interesting. The manufacturer of the drink brings his ware back to the village, and there sells it to one of two wholesalers for thirty pesos a gallon. Payment is made either in cash or in credit at one of the stores where the purchases of the _mescalero_ will be paid for by the wholesaler. The purchaser of the liquor sells it retail himself, or in bulk for forty pesos a gallon to various households that do a small business in vending the drink at retail. The retail price is one peso for about two ounces, and the majority of the retail sellers are the wives and mothers of men who make the drink. The _mescal_ maker usually keeps some of his product for his own use and to supply retail customers, but the bulk of his produce usually has to go to provide cash, either to settle an old account at the store or to make new purchases. When his personal supply is gone he finds himself in the position of a retail customer, slaking his often frequent thirst at a peso a drink.

There are thirteen households in the town that gain most of their income from the production of _mescal,_ and an additional five households where the sale of the drink provides some part of the income. Not including those households where _mescal_ is sold but not made, there are seventy-nine individuals in the village who are supported during the dry months by the produc-tion of the liquor. Twenty-seven of the town's eighty-six man work force (men over sixteen) engage primarily in _mescal_-making; one hundred and ten people in the village are associated with households where _mescal_ is either made or sold.

The use of the _mescal_ plant and the manufac-ture of the beverage are old customs in the valley. The aboriginal use of the plant as food appears to have been a characteristic here, as it is over most of the greater Southwest (Beals 1932: 103, 168-169), but its use to make an intoxicating liquor before the coming of the Spanish is unlikely. _Mescal_ was distilled and used in this section of Sonora as early as 1763, and then, as now, it was thought to have wondrous properties; "I have heard . . . that this liquor is remarkably efficacious as a remedy applied externally, for wounds, abscesses caused by blows or falls . . ." (Guitéras 1951: 38). Another report states that the Opatas learned to distill from the Spaniards. They also were described as having an insatiable appetite for the drink (Treutlein 1949: 177). Hrdlicka does not report the manufacture of _mescal_ in the region in 1902, yet he describes the Indians of the Río Cañon valley as drinking " . . . much Mexican mezcal or other liquor" (Hrdlicka 1904: 74). One is led to suppose that then, as now, the local _mescaleros_ were not eager to discuss their occupation with strangers. In this reticence they are joined by the villagers who do not engage in the trade, but who feel that the occupation is a blot on the village's reputation.

Making _mescal_ is a low prestige occupation. It is said by some of those who do not make it that no respectable household would allow either its manufacture or its sale by household members. Yet it is also said that at one time or another almost all males, particularly while youths, have made the beverage. _Mescal_ is sold in one of the most respectable houses, and in others of people who, though not of the highest prestige, are con-sidered to be quite upstanding. The greatest stigma apparently attaches to the manufacture of the beverage for subsistence purposes, rather than to the handling of the liquor. Making _mescal_ is disesteemed—selling it is a legitimate, if not highly regarded, method of obtaining income.

WAGE LABOR AND SPECIALIZATION

FOR THOSE without sufficient land or cattle to assure an adequate income, wage labor may provide supplementary income. Such work is usually associated with the fields and the employers are those who have too much land to be handled by their families alone. Agricultural work is intermittent here as elsewhere, with the great demand for laborers coming at planting and harvest times and little work being available during the growing season. Even with cotton, which demands much greater care during the growing season than either wheat or corn as grown here, the need for wage laborers is slight. This is due to the number of people farming shares in cotton on extremely small pieces of land. On such small holdings the household members of the share farmer can handle the necessary weeding, irrigating, and most of the picking. Several families have left the village to work in other parts of Sonora, particularly the area around Caborca, and some of the men have gone to the United States.

The average day's pay for a wage earner is ten pesos. Some skilled individuals, such as the tractor driver, earn up to fifteen, and immature youths and those working at jobs which require no skill are paid eight. Some men with a skill manage to obtain several days work each week and are nearly able to so support themselves. Others without such skills work only when some project is underway which requires several men, such as digging a well, and during peak seasons in the agricultural cycle. Many of the men who engage extensively in the *mescal* trade work intermittently at wage labor to supplant their income.

The only full-time specialists in the village are the school teacher and the man who tends the largest store. Even part-time specialists are rare. Most men engage in the various ways of making a living discussed above, and most men can do most of the jobs required in the village or in the fields. The only man practicing a trade is the blacksmith and even he has a number of other jobs at which he works — mailman, civil and criminal judge, carpenter, housebuilder, gunsmith, and others. Other men make adobes, run the motors associated with the wells, work at house building, cut hair, make leather lariats, and other such occupations required by life in the village. None of these men work at any of the trades more than intermittently, and all of the skills are shared with many other men in the town.

Women work around the house, take care of the children, wash clothes, draw water, and cook. Some women cook small items for sale around the community, bread, tortillas, tamales, etc., but only one woman does this regularly. She makes bread for sale each day, and her children take it around from house to house offering it for sale. Two women offer meals to travelers for a small price, but visitors to the village without friends with whom to eat are rare. When corn, beans, and wheat were the major items cultivated, women did little work in the fields. With the advent of cotton last year everyone who wished to pick the crop was so employed, including men, women, and children. Some of the poorer women take in washing and ironing, and some of these same women find temporary employment in the kitchens of the more well-to-do as cooks, or sometimes as nursemaids. A bundle of soiled clothes that may take all day to wash and iron earns for the woman around three pesos. A woman working in a kitchen all day may receive her meals and three or four pesos. Earning money through wage work in Marobavi is not easy for either men or women; the rates are low and the work is scarce.

COMMERCE

TWO STORES dominate commerce in the village, and both of these are owned by the same men who own the wells. Two other small stores are operated in homes but between them they probably do less than half the volume of either of the two main stores. Many other people sell small items in their homes such as soda pop, inexpensive shoes, seasonal fruits, canned foods, etc. These are picked up either on the periodic trips to other towns or are bought from salesmen passing through Marobavi and are then held until a demand develops for them within the village.

Both of the main stores are small, one-room establishments attached to living quarters and store-rooms. Each store has its clientele, most of whom are carried on credit on periods of from days to months. One store carries a considerably larger inventory than the other, and it does a correspondingly larger business. In one store or another it is possible to buy an amazing number of things including nearly every commercial item that plays a part in the daily lives of the villagers. Prices in relation to the daily wage of about ten pesos are extremely high, though the prices of such vital foodstuffs are low, as for example corn, beans, and wheat flour. Canned goods generally are about the same price as the similar item in the United States, though some are higher. Clothing prices have about the same range, but many articles of common wear sell in Marobavi for more than the retail price in the United States. The prices charged here are slightly higher than in Palo Fierro and considerably higher than in the non-valley towns. All goods must be trucked in, and it is not known whether this mark-up realistically represents increased operation cost or not. Many of the townspeople resent the prices charged and point to the advanced wealth position of the store-keepers as proof that an excess profit is made.

There is a small *cantina,* or bar, in the village that sells only beer. The *cantina* usually has a stock of beer not more than once a week. Beer, at a peso for a six ounce bottle, is expensive and demand for it usually follows some influx of money into Marobavi. The *cantina* opens for all the major fiestas, and for those of most importance ice is brought from Tomchic to chill the beer. The machine to produce music (generator, amplifier, turntable, and speaker), is usually located here and the *cantina* furnishes more music to the town than it does beer. Almost every evening young men, paying a peso a record, keep the machine in operation for several hours at a time. For a peso the patron chooses his record and is allowed to make a dedication over the loudspeaker system to either the girl of his choice or to one of his male friends. When record play-

ing at a peso a record, and beer drinking at a peso a bottle are combined it is possible to spend a large sum of money in a short time. One eighteen year old, returning from his first trip to the United States, kept the turntable going and several friends intoxicated for a period of five or six days. At the end of this time all of his savings were gone but he had put nearly every man in the village in his debt, and had serenaded every young lady in the area. The *cantina* is owned by two young men who operate it as a side-line; both engage in agriculture as well.

CLOTHING AND FOOD

ALL CLOTHING worn by the villagers is bought from the stores either as finished articles or as material from which to make items of dress. That of the men is identical to that worn by many rural men in the American southwest—boots or shoes, cotton twill trousers or blue jeans, cowboy-style work shirts or standard dress shirts, and hats made of straw styled after a conservative, fairly low-crowned and narrow-brimmed Stetson. Wide-brimmed *sombreros, huaraches, serapes,* and other features of dress associated with Mexico to the south are as foreign in Marobavi as they are in New York City, and because of the unfavorable stereotypes associated with *guachos,* or southerners, they would likely be regarded less favorably. The only article of clothing found here not common in the southwestern United States is a type of shoe made from deer or cowhide, and worn by the older and poorer men. This shoe has a standard shaped sole of stiff, hard leather, to which is sewn an upper of soft leather. Two pieces are used to sheath the foot, one covering the toes and instep, the other going from the instep, around the heel, and coming back on the other side. The two pieces are stitched together and sewn to the sole. A laced opening over the instep allows easy entry for the foot. This type of footgear, called locally a *tegua,* or moccasin, closely resembles modern style shoes.

Women wear some ready-made dresses but more commonly make their own from material bought at the store, brought home and sewn on the sewing machine, using fashions found in clothing catalogues as patterns. Nearly every home has a sewing machine and has had one for a long time. All of the machines are old and many no longer work. Women wear either lowheeled, lowcut leather shoes or rope-soled canvas slippers. Both of these types are usually bought at the store, though some women make their own *chanclas* or rope-soled slippers. Women's dress lengths vary between the knees and the ankles, and are worn longer as the woman grows older. Whenever outside the household area, and very frequently even when working in the kitchen, women's heads are covered by *rebezos*, or shawls, and even young girls are rarely seen in the streets without this head covering. *Rebozos* are usually homemade of lengths of material, either cotton or some acetate fabric, and may be a single color — white, black, blue, red, brown, or may be multi-colored, usually striped. Striped fabrics, even though containing many colors are usually somber in effect, and the black *rebozo* is very common, particularly for older women and widows. Shawls are worn over the head with one end hanging down in front, the other thrown back over the shoulder passing under the chin, thus framing the face. When planning on spending some time in the hot sun women occasionally wear a standard men's hat in addition to the *rebozo*.

There is little in the dress of the inhabitant of Marobavi to distinguish him or her from the poorer people found in the towns and cities of northern Sonora. Nor is there much to identify the wealthy in the village from the poor. All wear about the same style clothing and though initially they may differ as to quality, after a few washings little difference remains in appearance. Excluding the children of one storekeeper who wear clothing bought from the larger stores in the next valley, all of the children dress as do their elders. Only very young children belonging to the poorest families are allowed ever to go about without clothes, and most children by the time they are three are almost exact copies of their parents, even to the shoes. The expense involved in dressing growing children becomes prohibitive for the poorest families, however, and these children more often are seen wearing old and ill-fitting garments, and going barefoot.

The diet of the villagers centers around *frijoles*, or beans, potatoes fried or boiled, wheat and corn tortillas, eggs, and some meat. *Frijoles* are usually boiled and sometimes re-fried, and are served at every meal along with wheat *tortillas;* the two in combination often are the only food taken at a sitting. Three meals are eaten each day, early in the morning, noon, and mid-evening. Those working near the house, and children and women, have a piece of bread or a *tortilla* along with coffee in the mid-afternoon. Beef, when available, is roasted, fried, or boiled and made into a stew. Dried beef is invariably boiled and eaten in combination with various vegetables. Pork, even less often available than beef, is most frequently made into *tamales* (meat with chili surrounded by corn mush, wrapped in corn leaves and steamed) both to be eaten by the family and to be sold. Little milk or cheese is produced in the village and very little is imported. Only one man keeps cows within the village for the purpose of producing milk for sale, and the three which he does have rarely give more than a gallon between them on any given day. Seasonally, vegetables appear and provide variety in the diet; tomatoes, onions, garlic, and sweet garden peas are the most common, but none of these are always available and at times it is not possible to buy any.

Large quantities of coffee are consumed, both at meals and between, and at an average price of sixteen pesos per kilo, it is a big item in everyone's budget. Coffee is usually drunk black with sugar. Various herb teas are used, those made of *cósahui, yerba buena,* and one made of orange peel are the most common. A beverage made of corn, and called *tesvín* is sometimes made, particularly in hot weather. *Tesvín* is made by adding *panocha* to a pot containing corn and water and allowing fermentation to take place. The result is mildly alcoholic, has a sharp, pleasant taste, and is considered to be a refreshing soft drink. In another form, called *tepache*, fermentation is allowed to continue longer and a drink of some potency is obtained. *Tesvín* was seen to be made by only one woman, and *tepache* was not made during the period covered by this study. Soda pop, very common in the village and also very cheap, may have made the production of *tesvín* appear laborious, and *tepache* would be in competition with the inexpensive and extremely potent *mescal*. Bottled soft drinks are taken frequently between meals by everyone, but like the alcoholic beverages, they are almost never served at mealtimes. One indication of the town's isolation is the absence of the all but universal Coca-Cola sign, nor is the beverage sold in the town.

It is likely that at one time or another every family in the community buys some of all the commodities it consumes, including corn and beans. Food storage, except for these two items, is almost non-existent, and even families that raise these two staples in quantity are often forced to buy additional when their supplies prove inadequate. Except at the stores, not a single room was seen devoted solely to the storing of food. Sacks of corn or beans occupy corners of kitchens or bedrooms, or they may be placed in a temporarily vacant house or room, but granaries or storage rooms *per se* are not found. The customary pattern seems to be to sell much of the crop for cash, and to store something less than will be needed during the coming year, making up the deficit by purchasing what is required at the time it is needed. This also applies to seeds. In some cases men had to purchase beans or corn to plant a crop though they had raised one the previous year.

HUNTING AND GATHERING

HUNTING and gathering activities add some variety to the diet, but in quantity, they do not add much to the table. Both cottontail rabbits and the larger hare or "antelope jack-rabbit" are hunted almost daily by someone, but as much for sport as for meat. As often as not the meat is given away by the hunter or the carcass thrown to the dogs. Deer are almost extinct in the area around the village and it is now necessary to go either to the mountains to the east of Marobavi or to the plains in the next valley to the west to hunt them. Occasional trips are made to both places, usually during slack agricultural periods.

There are about a dozen firearms owned by villagers, most being Winchester 1894 model .30-.30 caliber rifles and carbines. There are about five .22 caliber rifles as well. The larger caliber, due to the expense of its cartridges, is used only for deer and other large game. The .22 serves for all rabbits, wild pig, coyotes, and when necessary for the larger animals as well.

Gathering of wild plants and fruits takes place continuously, with those persons passing through the river bottom or desert often collecting as they go. The only gathering activity that is of economic importance in the village, aside from that associated with *mescal,* is the picking of the small, red, spicy berry called *chiltepín*. This berry, secured from a bush that grows profusely in certain areas of the hills to the west of Marobavi, matures in the fall and whole families from Marobavi move out of the village to the berry areas for as long as the crop holds out. The picked berries are sold to buyers and ultimately they are sold all over Sonora where they are highly prized for their "hot," spicy flavor. Other wild plants eaten are the greens from several types of field weeds, and *berro* or water-cress, that is picked in quantity from the river.

The diet of the town is extremely lacking in variety both of content and preparation. Completely absent are elaborate dishes with rich *moles* found in other parts of Mexico. The only distinctive item in the food inventory is the replacement of the common Mexican corn *tortilla* with the large, thin wheat product. A few canned meats are available at the stores but these are purchased and served only on special occasions. The traditional Sonoran dishes, *posole* and *pinole,* are not very frequently made,[10] though *atole* is still made and drunk by most of the villagers. The use of all of these corn dishes is greatest among the poor people of the town, as is the collection and consumption of the gathered food. The major differences in diet between the well-to-do and the poor is quantitative; all eat about the same things prepared in the same way. However, some have meat, rice, vegetables and other relatively expensive items more often than others.

HANDICRAFTS

THE VILLAGE has no handicrafts as such. Within the last twenty years the making of palm baskets and hats, common to this part of Sonora (Johnson 1950: 14), has died out in Marobavi. In the village there still remains a pit where a *huúki,* the semi-subterranean round room used for making basketry by the Opatas, was once located. This type of basketry—plaited, square cornered, open topped—is still made in the valleys to the east, and a very similar type is manufactured by the Tarahumara Indians of Chihuahua. Those in use in the village now have all come from Tomchic or from the other valleys. The woven palm hats are highly valued all over Sonora for their durability, and in Hermosillo bring as much as a hundred pesos each. Some of the older women in Marobavi say they know how to make both hats and baskets but do not do so because the palm is no longer available in this area.

Some pottery is made in Marobavi for personal use, but very little is ever sold. It is made by the town's older women, and in the spring of 1955 only five or six women produced any at all. The feeling around the village is that when these women die, so will pottery making. Even now a woman living above Pueblo Antiguo supplies most of the large vessels used in all of the nearby towns. The pottery made by the women of Marobavi is a coiled and scraped, unslipped redware, made from clay found abundantly in the area and tempered with ground-up sherd materials.[11] New pieces of pottery are highly esteemed during the hot summer months because of the cooling effect on the water due to the evaporation that takes place through the slightly porous walls. Evaporation appears to slow down or stop as the olla is used for a while, so some women make new ones each year.

In addition to the pottery, a few items of wood are carved, trays or *bateas* and wooden spoons are the most common. The trays are used in the kitchens to hold *tortilla* dough while it is being prepared, and to hold the meat of freshly killed animals. Many of them are large, three or four feet long by two feet wide, and all are carved from a single piece of wood. Though shapes vary, most are slightly concave, thin at the ends and thick in the middle where the four stubby legs are located. Only a few men carve these and none are made currently. It is said that suitable trees from which to cut wooden disks for the *bateas* are no longer to be found near the village. Both pottery and the articles made of wood have been almost completely replaced in the homes by the common blue-enameled metal-ware.

Many houses have large copper cooking vats, often three or four feet across or more. These, of unknown origin, are used to wash in and to cook large quantities of food—one is nearly sufficient to hold an entire cow. It is possible that these vats were used in sugar cane refining.

WEALTH AND POVERTY

IN MAROBAVI there are extremes of wealth and extremes of poverty. The two rich families own stores, trucks, farm machinery, land, cattle, and mechanized wells; the poorest families have nothing beyond the wage earning potential contained in their bodies. The rich families have come to Marobavi within the last ten years, and both came either with large capital or with it available to them. The more successful of the two, a step-son of the wealthiest man in Palo Fierro, now has an estimated capital investment in the town of around 200,000 pesos, including a store, land, two mechanized wells, a truck, a tractor, and cattle. If the poorest individual in the valley were to dispose of all his possessions it is unlikely that he could raise one hundred pesos.

The villagers, in discussing relative wealth positions of the households, dichotomize between the rich and all of the other families in the community. This points to the fact that though there are gradations of wealth in the community among those native to it, the difference between any of them is not so great as that which separates all of them from the store owners. This difference not only refers to wealth position and point of origin, but also to basic motivations. The rich are interested in speculation, profit, and re-investment; the remainder of the villagers are concerned with subsistence and the necessities of life. The former view Marobavi as a place to be exploited, the latter view it as a place in which to live. The villagers lump the two families together and call them "los ricos," and contrast this term with "los demás" or "the rest of us," or just plain "we."

Excluding the two rich families, the rest of the villagers may be described, economically, in three groups. These groups do not represent distinct strata. There is a continuous gradation from poorest to richest, yet the villagers isolate three descriptive categories. (1) At one end of the continuum are about ten families who, through land ownership, cattle, small stores and other sources of income, are thought by the other villagers, and themselves, to have enough money to live more or less comfortably. These families live in the better houses in the village, work their own land, do little wage labor, do not engage in *mescal*-making, and have sufficient land or cattle to provide work for all or most of the children of the household. (2) Strongly contrasting with this group are about ten families who have little or nothing; no land, no cattle, live in small, poor houses, and either make *mescal* or engage in wage labor for subsistence. Several of these households were reportedly without food on some days during the period of this study. In some of the houses of people in this category the only items

of value noted were steel tools and a burro or two. Seven of these households are dependent on *mescal*-making, supplemented by wage work for their income. Three are composed of old couples who have no visible means of support and are maintained by other villagers. (3) The bulk of the villagers, about forty households, are in the middle between these two extremes. Though they have difficulty in obtaining sufficient money for all the necessities, through land ownership or ownership of small quantities of cattle, by means of fairly continuous wage labor, or by retailing on a small scale, they manage to "get along," that is, to eat regularly. They are able to provide the household members with clothing, adequate shelter, and food.

As in many rural areas of Latin America, the differences in standard of living and scale of life between the wealthiest and the poorest do not reflect the differences, proportionately, in income levels between these two groups (Service 1954: 108-116). Where these differences become most marked is the differential participation in profit making ventures, in those endeavors where risk is involved for the participants. Only the rich and the more well-to-do of the native villagers engage in independent agriculture; all the rest of the town either farm *medias,* work by the hour or day for wages, or make *mescal*. Both the rich and the well-to-do are able to face a complete loss of a year's crop without being destroyed economically; the rest of the village have nothing to allow them to recover from such a blow.

4

THE SOCIETY

IN THE COURSE of the day's events an inhabitant of Marobavi interacts with other members of his household, with members of his extended family, and with other villagers, and with these people his contacts will be more frequent than with any non-villagers. Even the most geographically mobile individual spends the greater part of his time in the village, while there are some who have left it only a few times in their lives. Yet all but a very few of the inhabitants have strong and close relations with others not resident in the immediate area — relatives in Palo Fierro, friends in San Juan, business contacts in other valleys or in Hermosillo, and many others. A complete discussion of the society of Marobavi would necessarily involve all of these and ultimately would lead to a discussion of widespread, possibly national, status groups, e.g. "rural peasant," and from there to a discussion of the place of the Marobavian in a national class system (Whetten 1950: 29). Such a discussion is not within the scope of this paper. Recognizing that such extra-village ties exist, it is possible to describe and discuss the ways in which the villager's relations with other members of his community are ordered, the intra-village organization within which are played most of life's acts, if not all of the scenes.

HOUSEHOLD AND FAMILY

THE MOST COMMON social group inhabiting the household is the simple nuclear family, a married couple with children (see Table 3).[12] Combining these with those nuclear family groups lacking one adult member, plus those households headed by a married couple without children, there are thirty-five households built around the nuclear family living alone. There are no households consisting of extended families (two nuclear families residing in the same household), but there is a tendency toward matrilocal residence. Ten nuclear families either reside with a parent of the wife, or are residing in the same multiple unit, or are occupying the nearest house to that of the wife's family. Only one such case occurs with the family of the male spouse. No explanation of this was found. Informants' statements were to the effect that residence is neo-local.

In most cases the nuclear family is not only the basic social unit but the primary economic one as well. Land is owned by the members of the unit, both male and female, and such cooperative labor as takes place in agriculture is generally within the nuclear family—sons with the father. When the children of such a family mature and the family of orientation is exchanged for one of procreation, both members bring whatever property they may have. A few married sons still work the land of their fathers, but many who have no land of their own are farming *medias* with one of the rich, or engage in wage labor. Several sets of brothers live in the village and all engage in separate economic endeavors with, in two cases, very distinct differences in economic stature between the siblings. Insufficient data were gathered to say that such marked kin group independence in economic affairs continues in the less visible area than that of physical collaboration, e.g. shared capital, loans, etc., but within the village there are notable differences in apparent wealth between many sets of people closely related to each other.

Eight households are composed of unmarried women and their children and have no male spouse within the household. Four of these consist of a woman and her children only, two have one parent or more of the woman, and the other two are composed of women with illegitimate children and the illegitimate offspring of the children. These households are supported by the economic activities of the adult members and are among the poorest families in Marobavi. Such households spring from multiple causes. Some have resulted from the break-up of free unions between a man and a woman that were either of such short duration or of such a transitory nature that the participants were not considered married. Others stem from the promiscuity of the woman, and at least one is the result of a long standing liaison between a man and a woman who have never resided together but who have had three children. In the latter case none of the children bear the father's name, nor do they share in his relatively high wealth position. Many of the fathers of the children are known by all, including the children themselves, but in none of these families are the children recognized by the father's name. There are at least two cases where a woman with an illegitimate child has been later married to another man, and in both cases the father of the first child still resides in the village. The children are either known by the name of the present husband or continue to use the mother's maiden name.

The single dwelling households are often set off from their neighbors by distances up to fifty yards, and even neighbors living close to one another are separated by shoulder high patches of brush and large trees. Further acting geographically to isolate household from household is the wide-spread nature of the village. It covers nearly half a mile from end to end, effectively blocking close physical contact between households located at the extremes. Individuals, particularly women, may go for days or weeks without seeing other members of the community who live some distance away.

MARRIAGE

MARRIAGE PATTERNS in the village, as indicated by the composition of the households, are similar to those of rural Mexico in general (Whetten 1948: 375-377). Marriages are either legalized by a civil ceremony, sanctified by a church ceremony, sanctioned by both of these, or are free unions, where the couple resides together without any ceremony. In Marobavi, the ideal type is that sanctioned civilly first, then by the church, but both of these ceremonies may be preceded by a period of cohabitation. Charges for the ceremonies are only a few pesos each and the majority of the married villagers have had at least one of the two. Many couples who have had the benefit of neither ceremony are considered in the village to be man and wife after several years of a stable free union.

The ideal marriage age is said to be about twenty-five years for men and a few years less for women. However, many below this age are married and several beyond it are still planning on marriage. The youngest married woman in the village is fourteen, though this was a forced union and immediately after the ceremony the husband left Marobavi and has never returned. The next youngest bride is eighteen, and the next twenty. There are no married males under twenty. Choice of partners is entirely up to the individual, but is subject to greater or lesser parental pressure. A recent marriage took place between a daughter of an influential family and a youth who was cordially disliked by all of the girl's relatives. Nevertheless the wedding was given by the bride's family, and at some expense. The couple set up housekeeping in the village and has never been visited by any of the bride's male relatives, all of whom still refuse to speak to the husband.

Many marriages in the community have endured for thirty years or more, and there is an air of permanence even to the free unions. Only one case of spouse-changing has occurred in the recent past and the interpersonal relations of cohabiting pairs observed were notably equanimous. Wife beating, loud verbal arguments and gossip about unhappy marital relations were all but absent. Women, ideally, are subservient to men; one young man who has never been to the United States remarked that he could believe all that he heard about that country except that the "women give the orders." Yet in those households closely observed decision making was as often in the hands of the women as in those of the men. A woman, asked if her young daughter was to be allowed to make a trip to Hermosillo, re-plied, "Yes, but we'll have to ask her father."

There are at this time in Marobavi twenty-seven individuals considered to be illegitimate, that is, without a sociological father and with no patrony-mic. If those individuals born outside of marriage but now included in another nuclear family are counted, at least five other persons are added. No particular stigma attaches to illegitimacy either for the child or the mother, other than that which may be attached to the general status position of the female parent. Attitudes generally are sympa-thetic toward both the child and mother because of the almost certain attendancy of poverty to such a family. All of the women with such chil-dren are poor, and in all but one case they are from families that have been poor some time into the past. The fathers, as far as they are publicly known, are typically from more well-to-do fam-ilies, and the father of at least five children, by three women, is the wealthiest man in Marobavi. It is said in the village that if the girl is over fourteen years of age (the national legal marriage age for females), the father of her children has no economic or social responsibility whatsoever. If he does not choose to marry her or to support the children, the woman has no recourse. And it is obvious in the village, contrasting the high wealth positions of some of the fathers with the extremely low wealth position of the mothers and children, that little or no help is given by the male parent. Illegitimacy, and attitudes toward it in the village are summed up rather well by the remark, "Well, if a woman cannot have a hus-band, it is better to have children than to be alone," and this from a woman who, at seventy-nine, has never married nor had children.

KIN GROUPS

THROUGHOUT the valley one is impressed by the number of people encountered who prove to be related to acquaintances from other valley towns. The impression is gained that many, if not most of the inhabitants of the valley from San Juan to Palo Fierro, are related to each other more or less distantly by either genealogical or affinal ties. This certainly is true of Marobavi. The web of kinship spreads throughout the settle-ment uniting all but a few of the nuclear families into larger kin groups. Where genealogical kinship ends, marriage ties begin, and when no relation-ship exists, frequently there are the known but unrecognized relationships due to common pater-nity, or those established through ritual kinship.

There are thirty-five surnames carried by household heads in the town. Though only eleven are present in more than one household, this does not reflect the degree of kinship affiliation be-tween the various living units (see Table 2). The proliferation of surnames is due to many causes, and often masks strong kin ties between different family names. If a woman joins in a free union and has children, the children bear the father's name. If the father moves on he leaves his name behind, and if the woman has future children, they will have a different surname than their half-siblings. Other names are added to the village roster by the movement to the village of male spouses. At the present, eight family names are due to such a cause. Additional names are added by the movement into the village of whole families not related to any others, e.g. the school teacher, and by the two cases of unattached, elderly people, who have moved to the village to live. Ten surnames are shared by thirty-eight households, with thirteen intermarrying families represented, and though no prohibition exists barring marriage between people bearing the same surname, no such cases were found.

The family in Marobavi is bi-lateral; equal recognition is taken by ego of the kin of both parents. Names are inherited from the father, except in cases of illegitimacy, and the connective "y" is rarely if ever used to indicate maternal familial ties. Women, upon marrying, retain their maiden names and add the possessive adjective "de," followed by the name of their spouse, e.g. Rita Martínez de Valenzuela, where Rita Martínez is the woman's maiden name.

Whether they live together or not, close kin are often seen in each other's company and usually are quite close friends. There are less than ten households not closely related to at least two others genealogically. Two of these represent women who came to the village late in life and who live alone, another is that of one of the rich who has not married but who has unrecognized offspring in several households, another belongs to the school teacher, and the others are households about which incomplete data were gathered.

Ritual kinship, known to be strong in most areas in Latin America, appears to be poorly developed in Marobavi. The formal structure of the ritual kin system is apparently the typical one (Mintz 1950: 341), yet bonds formed by the god-parent relationship appear to lack the social importance associated with them in other areas. An individual may take god-parents at baptism, confirmation, marriage, and at least one other religious occasion, Holy Week. Individuals occasionally refer to each other by the ritual kin terms, *comadre* and *compadre,* but most do not use them. The only obligation stated to be incurred through such ties was for all people standing in these relationships to "respect" each other, but lack of respect characterized a few such relationships. It is possible that further research would demonstrate a much more important social role for ritual kinship than is assigned it here. During the period of this study, *compadrazgo* as a social force seemed less important than genealogical and affinal ties, general status, and other features to be discussed below.

STATUS AND RANKED GROUPS

LITTLE WORK has been done on the analysis of class in Mexico, and the relationship of the rural agriculturalist to the urban system of stratification is not known. It is possible that a national scheme would group all of the small subsistence farmers and *mescal*-makers of the Río Cañon valley into a rural lower class and only slightly differentiate the rich in the village from all the rest. While such a classification might be justified on the basis of culture content and shared values, nevertheless there is a system of stratification in operation in the village which, though it certainly does not demarcate social classes, recognizes several groups that cluster about points on the

continuum of prestige. The most easily recognized principles that allocate a position to a member of a household are three: (1) identification with the aboriginal group, (2) wealth position, (3) an intangible that might be called "character."

The physical types that are found in the village have been described above with the two extreme types referred to as "Indian" and "White." To what degree these physical types match the genetic fact could not be guessed, and is not really of crucial importance here. What is of importance is that the villagers do make distinctions on the basis of physical appearance, and use these criteria as one device for assigning prestige. Three classifications are made by the villagers; either an individual or a household is Indian, or it is White, or it is composed of *mestizos.* About one third of the villagers are assigned to each group (see Table 4) and most individuals and households do have the phenotype associated with their "racial" classification.

Skin color distinctions are made in Marobavi, but without many fine gradations. The terms used, "blonde," "red-headed," "light," "brunette," "dark," and "black,"[13] are about the same as those used by many upper-class Mexicans to designate skin color when no racial implication is involved. To be dark skinned in Marobavi is a mark of low prestige, and while not infallible as a status marker, skin color is the best single visible indicator of the position of an invidual on the status ladder of the village. The dark skin, unless controverted by some other factor, marks the individual as a descendant of the aboriginal group, and hence an Indian. The term *indio* or "Indian" is used sparingly in the village and then only as a term of reference, never one of address. The people classified as Indians use the term only in a self-deprecatory sense, "We're nothing but poor Indians." It is also used by these people, and others in the village, to voice displeasure with children, e.g. "What a dirty little Indian!" Whites often employ euphemisms in place of the term "Indian" to designate the people meant; "them," "those that live over there," and "the indigenous people" are the most common.

The people in the village when identifying

households as to their "racial" affiliations, assign twenty-four to the White category, seventeen to the mixed group, and eighteen to the Indian.[14] A cross tabulation of these households with the classification of household units by wealth position shows an extremely strong correlation between assumed racial background and wealth position (see Table 4). Only one of the well-to-do is considered to be Indian, and on the other hand, all but one of those considered to be Indian are in the two lowest economic categories. Those economically considered to be poor, the lowest economic group, are predominantly Indian. The congruency between the two systems of classification is almost perfect, varied only by one household described as well-to-do and as Indian, and by two households that are classified as mixed and poor.

These cases are instructive. The well-to-do Indian is a cattle owner and has land as well, and one of his sons is part-owner of the *cantina*. His brother and several of his children reside in the village and all are considered to be Indians, yet when people were asked what his affiliation was many replied that he was not an Indian, that he was well off, and furthermore his father had been of a well known White family. While his paternity may have been different from that of his brother, in other similar cases the paternity is ignored and the individual is classified in the same racial category as the mother. Of the two mixed households which are classified as "poor," the name of one was frequently mentioned as Indian, though the family is as European appearing as any of the households considered to be "mixed." This household, however, is extremely poor and is composed of a woman head, and two generations of "fatherless" children. The problem here seems to be the reconciliation of assumed racial background with the local association of Indian-ness with poverty, and White physical type with wealth. The problem is resolved by some through ignoring the overtly apparently physical criteria and locating the individuals and households in question by reference to status markers other than physical characteristics.

Several criteria in addition to physical type

define membership in the various status groups: land ownership, occupation, traditional familial association with the village, marriage patterns, house types, and others (see Table 5). None of these criteria completely sets off one group from another; it is, instead, a matter of frequency. The sole exception to this is that no White households contain members who manufacture mescal, but three White households do obtain part of their income from the sale of the beverage. The frequency of both manufacture and sale of the beverage is greatest among the Indian households. Land ownership is least common among the Indians, and only one of the eight households indicated as owning land among this group has enough to be considered among the families that are well-to-do. Most of the others find it necessary to engage in wage work or handle *mescal*. The poverty of many Indian families is further indicate by their material possessions and the house type in which they reside. Two-thirds of the Indians reside in *casas de dos naves*. Of the third who do not, many live in single room, flat-roofed abobe houses marked by the same absence of material possessions that characterize most of the other Indian homes.

Another feature that differentiates between many Whites and many Indians is that the Indians typically think of Marobavi as their ancestral home and have no remembrance or knowledge of their families ever having lived anywhere else. Half of the Whites are not native to Marobavi and many of these are from some distance away — Tomchic, Ures, other river valleys, or even from Hermosillo. One of the effects of this disparate origin is readily seen walking through the desert with various individuals. The Indians know the name of every plant and animal, the haunts of the bees and the site of every cave, and have a name for nearly every natural feature. Some of the Whites know most or all of these things, but many know nearly none.

Possibly related to differences in attitudes toward the village as a place in which to live and to work, are the relative numbers of the three categories who have gone to the United States to work. Few Indians have gone, and none are going now. If the figures on movement to other parts of Sonora were included in Table 5, the differences would become larger. In 1955 several White families and some of the mixed talked of going to Caborca or to the cotton camps around Hermosillo. Only one Indian family planned on moving, and then to the neighborhood of Tomchic, still within the valley, and planned definitely on returning in a month or two. All braceros need to carry a letter of recommendation from the president of the *municipio,* plus sufficient money to take care of expenses until the first paycheck is received. While most of the Indians would likely receive the necessary letter most would not have the required expense money. Still, to go as a wetback usually costs less, and very few have left in this way either.

Illegitimacy rates are higher among the Indians than the Whites, and consequently there are more female-headed households among the former group. Economically this type of household is at a distinct disadvantage even if the woman herself once owned property. Without adult males to work the land and bring in cash and food, the land is soon lost through sale or mortgage, and in either case no longer contributes to the maintenance of the family. This type of family has a built-in self-perpetuation mechanism: with the laissez-faire attitude that prevails in the village regarding illegitimacy and marriage, this type of household has little hope of forcing a marriage for a daughter with child. There are presently two households where a sociological father is absent for two generations back. While taking the census of the village an attempt was made to collect names and places of birth of at least two generations preceding that of the informant. In many cases where the identity of the mother and the mother's mother came easily, similar questions regarding the identity of the father were greeted with a laugh and a shrug, or by a remark that fended off the question. If the problem of illegitimacy were to be studied exhaustively in Marobavi, it is suspected that the incidence would be much higher than it herein appears.

It is possible to discuss and describe the status groups in Marobavi in terms of their differing characteristics, yet these are selected criteria, and the people who differ from others in some regards are identical to each other in many ways. People classified as "Indian" and those in the status "White" share the great bulk of their behavioral patterns, differing in only a few. Indian and White share more and have fewer differences with any person in the "mixed" category, than with an individual located on the opposite polar group. The status system is clearly not based purely on racial differences. The cases of the individuals of disputed placement indicate that economic position is also a strong factor in the social placement of members of the community. That economic mobility is a possibility, if a rare one, is demonstrated by the well-to-do Indian; that it may also be downward in direction is suggested by the "poor" household that is only sometimes placed in the Indian category.

Another type of mobility appears to be associated with that diffuse quality called here "character." Several individuals from poor Indian families are highly respected and treated with some deference by all, including the Whites. One of these is a man about forty who lives in the poorest house in the village, makes *mescal,* and lives in free union with a woman who had had two children out of wedlock to another man. This man would provide an excellent norm for the low status male in Marobavi, yet he is respected and spoken of as a man who is highly industrious, sober, but very unlucky. The blacksmith is another case of prestige assignment being based on other than economic-racial criteria. Coming from a "mixed" family and still strongly identifying with the Indian group, he has been elected village judge for several years past and is, by consensus and self-admission, one of the most influential men in the town of Marobavi.

"Character" as used here, is related to esteem, that is, the social reward accruing to an individual for fulfillment of his roles. But it is also more than this. It were as if the group had certain expectancies regarding the personality characteristics associated with the high prestige statuses, hence the degree to which any individual fulfills these expectancies is another factor in his social placement. Those individuals who approximate the cultural ideal in this respect achieve high prestige regardless of the other status criteria they may possess.

SOCIAL BEHAVIOR

IN ADDITION to the attitudes and values that tend to separate the status groups, very real barriers to intensive interaction exist in the economic and social behavior of members of the racial-economic categories.

The concern of the rich with the outside commercial world, their economic ties with people from other villages and towns, and their kinship affiliations which are also outside of Marobavi all tend to remove them from intensive interaction with most of the other villagers in every day life. Though they spend much time in the village, most of their relations with other villagers are impersonal in nature — employer, seller, person who can do favors, and always economic superior. The few close personal ties these men have in the village, aside from those based on a sexual relationship, are with men from the well-to-do group of the native townspeople.

Excluding the rich, the rest of the villagers are united by common interests in subsistence activities, village social affairs, kin and affinal ties. The well-to-do, some with personal, non-economic relationships with the rich, also have strong ties with the remainder of the land owners and cattle raisers in Marobavi through agricultural affairs. The landowning group, including all of the upper, or well-to-do strata, and most of those who merely "get-along," is characterized by strong genealogical ties, and by those created by marriage as well. An examination of kin ties within the landholding group shows that here physical type is a potent social factor. The White families in the village, of whatever economic position, are in almost all cases more closely related to other White families than to any which are considered to be Indian. Households tend to be more closely related to those other households of approximately equal economic standing than to those dissimilar in this respect. However, when the physical element is introduced the statement

has to be revised; households tend to be most closely related to those households which display similar economic and physical characteristics. Thus a White, well-to-do household in the village is more closely related to the other White, well-to-do households than to any other group in Marobavi. At the same time this household is closely related to many households of lesser economic standing, but is more closely related to those which are classified as White than to those classified as Indian. In the middle economic group those classified as racially mixed are about equally related to Indians and Whites, and primarily engage in wage work or are small scale agriculturalists. The status positions filled by people of the middle economic and racial groups effectively tie together the two polar extremes, and are characterized by a blending and mixing of those criteria used to describe the Indian and White statuses. Thus, through a chain of common economic interests, common racial background, and through kinship ties, the lowest prestige groups are connected with the highest native prestige groups. A poor Indian *mescal*-maker has common occupational interests with those *mescal*-makers who are "mixed," and genealogical ties with those Indians who engage in agriculture. The "mixed" *mescal*-maker often has strong kinship ties with those Indians who engage in agriculture, and both of these have close ties with some members of the upper, White group, the former through actual kin ties, the latter more often through common economic interests. One of the most common mechanisms which draws together the different status groups is that of marriage; high status males marry low status females and, at least in one case, the reverse has happened.

Economic relationships between all of the villagers, with the exception of members of nuclear family groups, are impersonal in nature. Two men jointly making *mescal,* keep separate those heads collected by each, and the money received for the run of the beverage is split proportionately. Cooperative labor in the village is usually done through the medium of wage labor. An individual needing help to work on an irrigation ditch employs his friends and other members of the village for so much per day. Even brothers deal with each other in monetary terms; if one has some item the other wants or needs, the object is as likely to be sold as lent. Relations between the various economic strata and common interest groups are also marked by this same impersonality, often motivated by a well developed concern with self-interest. In the fall and winter of 1954-55, several men, including a few of the well-to-do, were farming *medias* in wheat with one of the rich, the latter providing water from his well. After a prolonged drought, when water was urgently needed by the wheat grower, the well-owner decided that there was insufficient surplus water for the wheat lands and all the share farmers lost their crops along with their invested seed and labor. It was said in the village that the water was denied the wheat growers to force them to remove the wheat and re-plant cotton. Whether this was the actual motive or not is uncertain, yet the refusal of the water did force the wheat growers to re-plow their fields and plant cotton. When the cotton was planted, the water from the wells was sufficient to irrigate it.

The two most common meeting places in the village are the largest store and the home of the Indian *mescal* wholesaler, the former habituated by most of the men in the village, the latter by middle and low status male adults and by most of the male youths of the community. In the evenings men gather at both places and also at the home of an old White widow who runs a store. In her home upper status males gather to play cards and to drink, to discuss business and just to talk, and their group is usually surrounded by several lower status individuals who are there to watch the card games and occasionally to join in the conversation. Also in the evenings small gatherings of men are to be found in the homes where *mescal* is sold. Men come in, order a one peso glass, pass it first to all present, and then, when it returns, drink what remains. At one time or another all of the adult males of the community may be seen in most of these places, yet in each the composition is about the same from day to day, and

in each, one or another of the status groups is dominant numerically most of the time. Ease and familiarity characterize a gathering when it is composed entirely of one status group, but the feeling changes to restraint and sometimes hostility when a person of markedly different status enters. During this study the introduction of cotton was causing stress, particularly between the rich and some of the small agriculturalists. Some of the latter would leave a group when one of the rich entered it. Interpersonal relations between individuals of markedly different status positions, when not mitigated by kinship ties, consist of conversational deference and politeness on the part of the social inferior, and levity and familiarity on the part of the superior.

The *mescal* wholesaler's house serves at all times as headquarters for the male youth of the village, regardless of the status of their families. Here all of the young men with idle time on their hands play cards, drink, or talk, and not infrequently shout at the girls who deliberately pass by. This town is also the meeting place for the *peloteros*, or the baseball team. Baseball has only recently become a diversion in the town, though it is widely played throughout the rest of Sonora. Next to drinking it is now the number one amusement of the male youth of Marobavi as well as for many of the younger men. It is enjoyed as a spectator sport by all the inhabitants. The players, representing nearly every household in the village and nearly all who wish to play, view the game primarily as a form of amusement rather than as a competitive sport. This attitude is strikingly different from that held by the members of Palo Fierro's team, and when the two play Marobavi is usually badly beaten.

Nearly every Sunday and on many Saint's days, evening dances are held in a cleared area in front of the house of the village *mescal* wholesaler. They are usually attended by all of the male youth in the village and most of the female youth of the lower status families; girls from the upper status households attend intermittently. Behavior of the participants at the dances is very formal. Boys and girls who during the day chat and laugh freely together, often barely speak to each other at the dances. Waiting for the music to begin, the girls sit together on a log on one side of the dance floor while the men mill about around the edges of the cleared area. When the music begins, the men rush to choose their partners, return to the dance floor and then proceed to dance as if it were an obligation and a duty. When the music is over the man escorts the girl back to the log and there leaves her. While dancing the partners maintain solemn faces, and rarely does conversation pass between the dancers. All of the girls are escorted to the dance by their mothers who take seats behind the log used by the girls and from there observe the entire affair. A few married women occasionally attend the dances, but rarely dance. Most married men come, usually without their wives, and most of them dance frequently.

A few other organized amusements are sometimes provided by traveling shows that make their way through the valley visiting each of the small towns for a day or two. Possibly one or two of these, consisting of vaudeville-type acts, stop in Marobavi each year.

Drinking *mescal* is part of the normal expected behavior of a man in this community. Getting drunk, if done only a few times each year and neither accompanied by fighting nor extended over a long period, entails no gossip nor loss of prestige. Drinking, however, once begun is apt to last anywhere from one day to a month or more, and may ultimately involve wandering from one valley town to another. The return to the home village is finally brought about by the complete exhaustion of available assets, horse, saddle, boots, etc., with which to buy *mescal*. During these periods of drinking, men become openly gregarious and often boisterous, and travel about in groups of two or more, often on a single horse, documenting their location and condition with song. It is a rare day in Marobavi when there are no *borrachos* about the streets, and when the major fiestas occur all but a handful of the men of the village get drunk. Many women do not drink and none was ever seen drunk.

One is struck by the overt, social disassociation of the village adults from one another, that

is, except when drinking. Women, leaving the house only with some formal reason, may go for days or even weeks without seeing other women living nearby. Doña Tula, an active woman in her seventies, has a son and daughter-in-law living about one hundred yards away but so located that the two houses are not visible from each other. Periods of weeks pass in which the two women do not exchange words. All news passed between the two households is carried by the male members and the children. The solitary horseman is a common sight in the area as is the man working alone in the fields. Though men circulate more freely than do women they most frequently do so alone. At night men may move from one social gathering to another but they come in by themselves and leave the same way. Close friendships appear to exist between youths of the same age and sex. Many pairs and threesomes are seen almost continuously in each other's company, and these small sets of friends often combine into larger groups characterized by warmth of feeling toward each other. Whether these friendships in another form are continued into later life is not known. If so, the overt manifestations change as the youth turned adult moves into the more family-centered activities of adult status. The formerly close companionship with many of the peer group becomes a different type of relationship, possibly that of ritual kinship.

It is rare to see close friendship between youths of families from widely separated status groups. All of the youths of the community mix during leisure time activities without any apparent regard for social criteria that may set their families apart, yet when these larger aggregations split into pairs or threesomes the individuals contained within each of these small sets are usually from families in more or less the same social position. That this represents any snobbishness is doubtful. Instead it probably reflects many of the same forces that act to group adults together in daily life; common occupations, common economic interests, common expectations, kinship ties and similar leisure schedules.

CIVIL OFFICES

IN MAROBAVI there are two civil offices representing the *Municipio* and ultimately the federal government. These offices are the *comisario de policía* or police officer, and the *juez civil y criminal* or civil-criminal judge. How men are chosen to fill these offices is not clear; some informants say they are elected, others say they are appointed. The way in which it seems to occur is that individuals are informally nominated and their suitability for the office is then discussed in the village. When the election takes place little doubt remains as to who will attain the office, and the ultimate sanction to hold the position comes from the *presidente municipal.*

The police officer has little to do in Marobavi and the office carries little responsibility. His primary duties are concerned with the promulgation of official notices sent to Marobavi from Palo Fierro, and the maintenance of the peace when it is threatened. This office has been held by many of the adult males in the past and the chief qualifying factors are reliability and moderation in drinking habits. The office is presently held by a relatively poor Indian who has since gained stature in Marobavi due to his position. He has, however, only moved from a low prestige status to one somewhere nearer the middle. He formerly drank a great deal and made *mescal*— now he does neither.

An office presently with more power in the village than that of police officer is that of civil and criminal judge. It is the judge who decides who is to be punished for what and how severely and, in fact, is the actual voice of the *municipio* in the village. Very little happens in Marobavi, however, that cannot be settled without recourse to formal authority. During the period of this study possibly five men were sent to the jail for a period of a few hours each, all for drinking excessively and fighting. A slightly more complex case was presented when someone burned down the dance ramada used on San Isidro's day. The culprits were soon found when it was remembered that two youths, neither of whom smokes, were borrowing matches. They both were fined a few pesos and made to pay for the destroyed beams.

Another civil office, not formally linked with the *municipio* structure, is found in the village. This is the *juez de campo,* or judge of land-use, who is elected by all those villagers owning land or cattle. It is he who regulates the use of the small amount of existing river water, allocates the use of the non-cultivated land, and whose approval is necessary before any major change may be made in the present use of land in the Marobavi domain. The man now holding the office is White, well-to-do, and possibly the most respected man in the village.

5

RELIGION

LITTLE is known of the religious beliefs and practices of the aboriginal inhabitants of the *Opatería*. The early missionaries, accustomed to the highly organized and complex religions of the southern Mexicans, were led to remark on the lack of religion among the Sonorans (Guitéras 1951: 58-64). It would be surprising if the Opatas, described as culturally superior to all their neighbors, had any less complex a belief system and religious organization than had the aboriginal Yaquis. Beals describes a pantheon, a number of religious specialists, and a long list of ceremonials for the Yaquis prior to Spanish contact (Beals 1943: 57-71). Whatever were the beliefs and practices of the Opatas, few if any religious customs remain that may definitely be tied to the pre-conquest times. The Marobavian is a carrier of the type of Christianity introduced into the area by the Jesuit and Franciscan frailes, and due to continuous if not intensive contact with priests until the present, religious practices have been constantly modified in accordance with changes in church teachings in the rest of Mexico.

THE CHURCH

THE CENTER of religious activity in the village is the church building, a flat-roofed adobe structure which is in a state of poor repair. The rear section of the roof and a room to the east of the altar have both collapsed and the edifice consists of a wall shell and a portion of roof that covers the north end where the altar is located. All of the churches in the valley from Palo Fierro to La Paloma are in about the same condition. Sporadic attempts are made to repair all of them by the respective villagers. The church at Palo Fierro is slowly being re-roofed with galvanized iron. Neither the exterior of the church in Maro-

bavi nor the interior is imposing. The flat exterior relief is broken only by the low bell supports found over the door; the interior walls are rough and consist of unfinished adobes plastered and whitewashed only on that section located under the roof. The low, plain altar is usually covered with a white cloth and has above it to both sides images of the Virgin, Christ, San Isidro Labrador (the village patron), the Sacred Heart, plus two or three small, framed pictures. The church and all of its contents are thought to belong to all the members of the village rather than to the organized Catholic church.

The churches in Palo Fierro, San Juan, and La Paloma were old when Father Kino passed through the valley in 1687 (Bolton 1948). They were built sometime around the year 1650 but, due to continuous remodeling and repairing, it is likely that very little still remains of any of the original structures. The age of the church building in Marobavi is uncertain; various informants say it was built about 1890 and others are sure it was very old at that time. From Jesuit accounts there does not appear to have been a church in the village during the 18th century.

RELIGIOUS ORGANIZATION

THERE IS NO resident priest in Marobavi and none nearer than Tomchic to the south of Palo Fierro. This priest makes from two to four visits to Marobavi each year and visits Palo Fierro somewhat more frequently. His most regular visit to Marobavi is on the *Fiesta de San Isidro Labrador* (May 15th), when he says Mass, performs marriages, and baptizes children. Other visits are occasioned by notices to him that there are children to be baptized or couples to be married. All of the priest's services have a charge ranging from ten pesos for a baptism to fifty or more for a Mass on a major feast day. This money is either paid directly by the recipient of the service or, as in the case of a Mass, it is collected by one of the female villagers from the more devout members of the community. Presently there is some anti-clerical feeling in the village and it is directed more at the present priest than at the clergy in general. It seems to stem from the attitudes of this priest, who has been in the district only a few years, toward the village. He reportedly refuses to eat or sleep in Marobavi due to a lack of adequate facilities and berates the villagers for drinking, failure to support the church, for some of their religious practices, and for attending Protestant services. In addition, he has recently raised his fees.

In the daily religious life of the community the priest has no part. Only his ability to baptize makes him indispensable to the villagers. Religious routine is handled by a group of four women assisted by one or two others. This entire group is known as *las cantoras* or the singers. The *cantoras* are not a formal organization, there are no rules governing membership, no recognized leader, and no true area of recognized authority. Membership in the group appears to last until a person is incapacitated by old age, and selection to the group is at this time by invitation of the incumbent *cantoras*. Two of the women are from households most consistently identified as Indian, the other two are from the household only sometimes identified as Indian. All of the *cantoras* and their helpers are from poor families, three being from households composed of women with fatherless children. All but one of the *cantoras* have illegitimate children.

This group of women leads the singing in the church and in the religious processions. They are also taxed with the organizational work connected with the presentation of any religious service, and appear to direct every religious affair that takes place in Marobavi. But all of this responsibility, except for a few periods of intensive religious activity in the yearly round, requires at most not more than a few hours each week from each of the *cantoras*.

The old woman who takes care of the church is another part-time religious specialist. An Indian woman, it is she who is entrusted with the keys to the padlock that secures the front door of the church. She also dusts and sweeps inside and directs the activities of other women who help her in these chores. This woman, who is extremely poor, is not recognized by the present priest as a person of special status. Her job has no title, and holding it does not enhance her prestige in the village except in those affairs directly connected with the church. When this woman was younger she was a *cantora* but, having lost her voice, she no longer sings. How she was selected for the job is not known, but she will hold it until too old to perform it. She is now nearly eighty.

The only other permanent religious organization in the village is a group of young, unmarried girls who work in the church and attend to the religious instruction of the younger children. This group is unnamed and, at one time or another, young girls from nearly every family in the village were seen sweeping or cleaning within the church.

In the yearly ceremonial round at least two transitory organizations come into being: the *Fariseos* associated with Lenten observances (Owen, 1958), and the *Pastores,* a group of young boys and girls who dance for a fiesta in January, probably Epiphany, January 6th (see Table 6). It is possible that other short-lived religious organizations exist and come into action on particular feast days.

The *fariseos* are a group of young men who represent the forces of evil during the latter part of Lent, particularly during the last few days of Holy Week. This group is directly under the control of from one to four captains appointed by the *cantoras*. The total group consists of from ten to twenty male youth or young men. Homemade costumes and masks are worn by all except the captains and, during their play acting, the *fariseos* are forbidden to speak except by using a small reed whistle carried in the mouth. During the last few days of Holy Week the *fariseos* are most active and spend several hours each day in costume and baiting the forces of good, e.g.

women praying in the church, participants in the religious processions, the statues within the church, and the church itself. They create disturbances around the village by chasing children, horses, and dogs, and in general by be-deviling the other villagers. Membership in this organization is part of the expected behavior of all the male youth of the village, and it is said that all of the men native to the village have belonged. Participation does not seem to stem from religious zeal as much as from the desire for amusement. During the time when the organization is active many of the men are continuously drunk, mildly abusive to those to whom they normally would show respect, and are allowed to carry out pranks that would usually not be tolerated. The rather severe whippings administered to the *fariseos* on Holy Saturday morning constitute an additional stimulus to participation in that it is assumed in the village that only fear of these whippings will keep a youth from "coming out" as a *fariseo*. Hence a young boy striving to reach adult status is forced to enter the organization or be judged not yet a man. Boys begin to participate at around the age of fifteen and may continue until thirty-five or more.

The *fariseos* come into being as an organization in the week preceding Holy Week, when they make the church ready for the coming ceremonies. They are active through most of Holy Week, and then for a few days after Easter when they dismantle the paraphernalia used in the church and in the processions. They then cease to function until the following year. The only indication of a once more complex organization is offered by the continual presence at all of the Lenten observances of an old man who just stands off at once side and watches. The *cantoras* and the *fariseo* captains continually go to this man for advice on what to do next, or on how things should be done. Justification of the role he plays in the ceremonies was offered by one of the *cantoras* who said, "He remembers how things used to be," and she later remarked that the old man was "chief" of the *cantoras* and the *fariseos*. It is possible that he and his role are remnants of a once more complex organization found

among the *fariseos* group (Johnson 1950: 39-40). Even now there are many close parallels between the Holy Week observances in Marobavi and those practiced by the Yaqui. For example, in Marobavi the civil government turns over all of its authority to the *fariseo* captains.

BELIEFS AND CEREMONIALS

THE RELIGIOUS belief system in the village is almost entirely Christian. Discussions with the most influential *cantora,* who is uneducated and untraveled, indicate that beliefs, particularly about Christ and his life, are the orthodox ones. Since she, along with printed texts, is the chief source of religious lore in Marobavi, her beliefs are most probably shared by all of the inhabitants. Life in general in Marobavi appears extremely secular, and few instances of magic, sorcery, witchcraft, or of taboos that play a part in daily life were encountered. That such beliefs do exist is virtually certain. However, the brief nature of the field research and a failure to explicitly elicit such data resulted in very little being collected. Unfortunately, no life crises were observed, i.e. births, marriages, deaths, etc., and observational data on this area of culture, where supernaturalism might be expected to play an important role, are completely lacking.

People in Marobavi often say that religion is something that should be taken seriously and treated gravely, yet only a small segment of the population conforms to such views and then only occasionally. Saint's days are times for feting those bearing the Saint's name with music from the *cantina,* with small parties in the homes, and with large quantities of *mescal* in the case of male youths or adults. Dances are held on most major feast days, and several times during Lent as well, and all these religious times provide occasions for indulgence in drink. When somber and sad behavior is called for, only the religious specialists, some of the older women and very few of the men, approximate the ideal behavioral patterns. When the fiesta is to be on a large scale, those at the conclusion of Holy Week and the three day celebration on San Isidro's day for example, many outsiders come to the village for fun, and the temporary food and drink stands set up in the plaza and the *cantina* all do a booming business.

Prayer services using printed texts read by one of the *cantoras,* and rosaries sung by a *cantora* with the other people in attendance responding, are the most common religious services. The number of such services (see Table 6) appears incongruous with the lack of concern with religious matters displayed by most of the inhabitants of Marobavi, and it is suspected that the services are more important for the social needs they serve than for their religious content. At these meetings, usually held in the evenings, only women attend and for many it is the only time they leave the immediate vicinity of the household for days at a time.

Two other religious practices found in the village are the taking of *mandas* or vows, and the wearing of a *hábito* or religious costume. Vows are made to the Saints or to Christ stating that if some request is granted, the grantee will follow a particular line of behavior. A common vow taken by women is one where the person promises to wear the *hábito;* men sometimes vow to enter the *fariseos* or the whippings which occur during Holy Week. After a woman makes a *manda* to wear the *hábito* and the favor is granted, she may then hire someone to wear the religious dress for her. Children and the poorer women in the village are the most frequent substitutes.

Most houses have either a few holy pictures in a corner of one room or a small altar with an image or two located along one wall. Few services are ever held in private homes and those which are usually take place in a home of one of the *cantoras. Velorios,* or wakes for the dead, are sometimes held in private homes. They usually last all night, and involve praying and singing. The hostess provides food for those who attend.

The major ceremonial periods in the village are Holy Week, the four days surrounding the fiesta of San Isidro, and Christmas Eve. Throughout the year the feast days of various Saints are observed with greater or lesser interest, depending on the number of individuals in the village carrying the particular Saint's name.

Two items found in the ceremonial life of the villagers are possibly of aboriginal origin; *pascola* dances done by the fariseos during Holy Week, and a ceremony, called *táguaro,* held Easter Sunday afternoon. The *pascola* dance, consisting of a rhythmic shuffling of the feet, is done by individual *fariseos* during their antics. The dances are done spontaneously by any given *fariseo* and need not be accompanied by music. The term refers only to the dance-step, not to the dancer, nor is there in Marobavi any formalization of the dance—it is casually done as part of the routine behavior of the *fariseos.* Spicer believes that the term *"pascola"* is of Yaqui derivation rather than Spanish (Spicer 1954a: 173-174), hence it is possible that the closely related Opata may have had a cognate form. In fact, the term was used circa 1765 to describe a dance in northern Sonora (Treutlein 1949: 181-182). It is also possible that the term, if not the step itself, has been introduced into the village by traveling Yaquis who are known to have put on *pascola* dances in Marobavi. This last suggestion is given weight by the failure of several of the town's oldest citizens to identify the term "pascola" as a dance. Many thought it referred to the activities of the participants in the *táguaro.*

The *táguaro,* though it is no longer remembered as such, appears to be a survival of an Opata scalp dance celebrating the taking of an Apache scalp (Hrdlicka 1904: 76-77). Easter Sunday afternoon, 1955, several of the men and youths who had taken part in the *fariseo* group, plus some who had not, dressed in women's clothes, painted their faces with bluing and lipstick, and disappeared into the brush in back of the village. The party included about fifteen men and boys in all. Near the church a long *carrizo* cane was set up and a small, carved figure placed on top. This figure, carved from a length of pitahaya cactus, was about eighteen inches long and humanoid in appearance. It was dressed in red crepe paper clothes under which was hidden a large erect phallus. The figure was treated most casually prior to being placed atop the pole. The carvers carried it about exhibiting it to all first covered by clothing, then while the viewer was contemplating the handiwork, the dress would be whipped aside displaying the phallus. Whatever the reaction of the victim, it would be followed by gales of laughter.

After the costumed group had been in the brush for about twenty minutes, adults of both sexes and children began to gather in front of the church. Men carried rifles and many were drunk, children began collecting animal droppings and piling them up, and the few women present just stood by. Suddenly the painted "Apaches" and "Comanches" dashed out of the desert and made a rush for the pole upon which was fixed the figure. As they came they shouted and jumped, made threatening gestures, and finally began to chase the children who were pelting them with dried animal dung. Children captured were carried out of the village. The whole Apache group retired after a few more minutes. In the two following attacks, coming about ten minutes apart, the Apaches and Comanches continued to attempt capture of the children, and more and more would dance around the pole. On the final pass all of the raiders danced under the pole and the male bystanders began to shoot at the figure at the top. Two or three dozen shots were fired and failed to dislodge the figure. Finally the *carrizo* pole was shaken by hand and the doll fell off. It was immediately snatched up, and with all of the participants in attendance, it was carried off to the spring just below Marobavi, and there baptized by god-parents previously chosen.

Scalp dances are reported for the aboriginal Opatas (Beals 1932: 192), but one described for the Opatas circa 1761 differs entirely from the contemporary *táguaro* (Guitéras 1951: 67-68). If the dance was originally designed to commemorate a victory over the Apaches, it certainly was begun during the time of the Spanish, or even as late as the 18th century.

RELIGIOUS ATTITUDES AND PARTICIPATION

PARTICIPATION in religious affairs in Marobavi lacks the quality of intensity noted in other Mexican rural villages. This report covers a period of time when the ceremonial cycle reaches its peak, yet attendance at any of the ceremonies and services rarely included as much as one-half of the population, and often less than one-quarter of the residents were present. Religious events are anticipated some weeks in advance and are discussed frequently, then passed over with little note taken of them by many of the people. Townspeople began to talk about the coming fiesta of San Juan two weeks before the date (June 24). Yet, when the traditional procession carrying San Juan's picture wound down to the river, there were about eighteen young girls, six adult women, and three men in the group. When the procession of Good Friday started out of the church door later in the afternoon, the men were playing baseball directly in its path. The baseball game stopped only long enough to allow the procession, composed of about thirty-five women and children, to pass, and then the game continued. One man stood up from where he had been watching the game and asked indignantly, "Is no one going to go?" Then he alone joined the end of the procession.

Men virtually never attend the weekly or daily prayer services, and even during Holy Week male attendance at any function appeared to vary directly with the potential for amusement the event was expected to have. When *fariseos* were expected many men came to watch; when the procession was to consist of the way of the cross only, men were conspicuously absent. About half a dozen of the high prestige villagers, all white and well-to-do or rich, were noted as not taking part in any ceremonies—all of these are men. At no ceremony were men, including those participating and those merely observing, much more than one quarter of the total group.

Male participation in religious affairs differs markedly according to the racial-economic group to which the individual belongs. When men do take part, fulfilling the needs of the various processions, they are almost entirely from households classified as Indian and as being poor. Most of those belonging to Indian households are more or less active in church affairs, even if merely as spectators. No person considered an Indian was an outspoken critic of the priest as were some of the Whites.

No such differential participation is found among women from households of the different status groups. All but one or two women in the village attend church more or less regularly, and at some of the processions during Holy Week all but about ten of the adult women of the village were present. Though Indian women dominate the formal religious statuses, the membership in the young girls' group is not restricted by family status. Many of the most active girls are from well-to-do families.

"Official" participation in religious activities does not bring high prestige in the village. Several of the *cantoras* are, in every-day life, treated with disdain by many White males; one *cantora*, the "leader" of the group, was seen to be pushed about by a man. These women are rarely accorded the respect title *"Doña,"* and in speech are often deprecated, particularly by White men. Even many of the Indians show them no particular respect in non-religious matters. Most of the *cantoras* are, on the basis of other criteria for prestige in Marobavi, candidates for the least amount of it in the village. All but one are Indians, all are poor, three have illegitimate children, all but one live in *casas de dos naves,* and all reside in households wherein *mescal* is made or sold. Their general prestige positions appear to be hardly, if at all, affected by the religious offices they fill.

Most of the men active in religious life are not in the generally depressed status positions whence come the *cantoras*. The semi-permanent captain of the *fariseos* is one of those individuals who, though exhibiting many characteristics associated with low prestige, is respected in the community for his personal attributes. In 1955, the two additional captains of *fariseos,* one from an Indian household, the other from one considered to be "mixed," were both men accorded some prestige. The old man who always hovers around the ceremonials, while treated with levity by many of the Whites, is accorded a measure of prestige by all and is shown deference by most of the Indians. Activity in religious affairs does not seem to have any noticeable effect on the prestige position for either men or women.

Overt devoutness in religious matters is rare in Marobavi. Even the *cantoras* seem to be as much concerned with the social aspects of the sacred life, as they are with God and the church. Only the old woman who takes care of the church building demonstrates a consistent interest in prayer, the welfare of the soul, and the sanctity of the place of worship. To her, the religious fiestas are times of processions, prayers, sadness, and joy. To the mass of the villagers they are times of dances, visitors, meals with meat, drinking, with a procession to watch in the afternoon. During Lent the customary Sunday night dances are always held, and some individuals remarked that, "Lent is sad in many places, but not here in Marobavi." The church building itself, in many parts of Mexico a sacred place, appears to derive its sacred character in Marobavi as much from the ceremonies taking place in it at a particular time as from any sacredness inherent in it. During the baseball games played in front of the church, one of the minor objectives of the sport is to hit the ball through the open roof of the structure. This has an unknown potential for destruction to the altar and the images the building contains; they could easily be damaged. When the ball goes in, men and boys swarm up the walls or under the door, and after the ball is retrieved, someone always remains on top of the walls to clown.

An extreme attitude toward the manifestations of religion in the village was illustrated by one man, a White, who dismissed the entire Holy Week ceremonialism as a holdover from the days of the aboriginals. He took no part in any of them. This slightly atypical attitude is, however, indicative of the dispassion with which many people view religion in their own community. Instead of being adherents to a traditionally-derived sacred area of belief and ceremonialism, many of the villagers view religion merely as another part of their contemporary existence to be either enjoyed or not depending on what else there is to do at the moment, or what entertainment value it is expected to have. Actual participation and attitudes are no doubt influenced by purely social factors. The control of the church offices by Indian households seems to have been the case in the past and will continue for some time into the future. All accounts of past *cantoras* describe them as Indian women, and presently all but one of those who help the *cantoras* are Indian women, and they presumably will fill any vacancies. This association of a type of activity with the lowest prestige group in the village limits participation by those at the top. Roles in the ceremonials are handed out by the *cantoras* and very often go to relatives, and though a well-to-do White could likely obtain any of them by asking, they do not seem to do so. Only one adult White "came out" as a *fariseo* in 1955, while at the same time several adults classified as mixed, and Indian, were among the group. This White, a man from Hermosillo, was chided by nearly everyone while acting as a *fariseo*. He is the lowest prestige male in the village classified as White.

Some of the attitudes held in the village toward religion and its role in life are illustrated by the village's reaction to Protestant missionaries. In 1953, a group of men representing two Protestant denominations started visiting Marobavi about once a month. How they were initially accepted is not known, but they were successful in renting a house in the village which they converted into a simple church. They began having prayer meetings centering around singing, with music played over a gasoline-powered record machine, and giving sermons dealing with non-denominational "fundamental" Christianity. All of the individuals of the missionary group, and they vary from meeting to meeting, are personally liked by most of the villagers and they are esteemed by most for the work they have done on some of the roads.

Though a core of resistance has developed, centered around the *cantoras* and their families, most of the villagers have no strong feelings either toward or against them. Their prayer meetings usually draw thirty or more people and they are often successful in obtaining two or three public protestations of faith. But in all this time they have been successful in obtaining only one conversion, and this from a man who had recently lost his wife and who was offered the opportunity to travel about Sonora with the missionaries. The many people who attend the services have done so to hear the singing and music and to take advantage of the easy friendship to be had at the meetings. It also provides relief for what would otherwise be a routine evening. Though the priest has scathed the Protestants during his sermons in the church, and the Catholic weekly sent to the village has printed articles denouncing them, no villagers asked could cite any major doctrinal differences between what they believe and what is taught by the missionaries. The major criticism made of the religion offered by the visitors is that it requires complete abstinence from smoking, drinking, dancing, and having affairs with women, "a person just could not belong to such a church as this."

6

CONCLUSIONS

IN 1902 Hrdlicka remarked of the Opata Indians of Sonora, "The tribe is disappearing in a manner exceptional among American Tribes—by voluntary amalgamation with the whites . . . " Johnson, in a summary report on this same group, published in 1950, remarks that the " . . . Opata have completely disappeared today as a cultural and ethnic entity."

This paper represents an attempt to describe the state of the acculturation process among the descendants of the Opatas in one small village.

Several possible results of the acculturation process have been suggested, one of which is that called "complete assimilation" (Redfield and others 1936; Spicer 1954b; SSRC 1954). "Complete assimilation" finds the culture of one group being replaced by that of another, the patterns of one culture being submerged within those of the other: "Although it is never fully realized, assimilation implies an essentially unilateral approximation of one culture in the direction of the other" (SSRC 1954: 988). If complete assimilation is defined as the process of nearly complete cultural transference, then Marobavi is an example of complete assimilation. Only isolated items of Opata cultural patterns remain, and none of these is central to the contemporary culture of the village. The Opata descendants are completely assimilated to Spanish-Mexican cultural patterns.

This examination of the society of Marobavi indicates that social relations, as well as all other cultural patterns, are in the Spanish-Mexican tradition. The descendants of the two parent societies are now integrated into a single system of connected statuses which form a single society in which there are no caste or caste-like relations. Nearly all households in Marobavi, and *all* that have temporal depth in the community, have basic genealogical or affinal ties with several others.

Such relationships are less intense between households at opposite ends of the wealth-ethnic continua, yet they are present; the inhabitants of Marobavi form a single society. However, the individuals are placed along the prestige ladder in such a way that ethnic background is one of the important criteria of social placement or prestige accumulation. No Indian is cited among the most respected members of the community. In terms of ascribed and achieved status, all Indians are rated below some Whites. The characteristics which define Indian status — dark skin color, low wealth position, various occupations — are accorded low prestige, sometimes even by those who fill the status "Indian." Thus, the cultural patterns practiced by the descendants of the Opatas are almost entirely drawn from European or other outside sources, but the prestige accorded corresponds to their assumed derivation from the aboriginal group. Although they may be said to be "completely assimilated" culturally, socially they are still paying a debt to their Opata forebears. Ethnicity is a definite factor in their social placement.

The question asked here is this: after the contact situation has occurred and the acculturation process has reached the point where it may be said of a group, "It is completely assimilated," does this statement describe *social* relations as well as more general cultural patterns? The answer drawn from these data is negative. It is apparent that the process of social assimilation progresses at a different rate from the process of cultural assimilation.

It might be profitable, in dealing with acculturational problems, to differentiate social processes from general cultural ones, if not in all situations certainly in those where the process is leading to complete assimilation. This study suggests that, after initial contact, the social adjustment of acculturating groups to each other is as varied as are the more general cultural responses, that social and cultural assimilation are interrelated, but do not necessarily coincide in time.

In conclusion, although the Indians in the Marobavi community are completely integrated into the village social system, they are denied access to the whole range of status positions in the society because of their assumed relationship to the lowly-esteemed aboriginal group which, culturally, has disappeared. The society consists of people who have many common understandings, no one segment being ignorant of any other segment's cultural behavior. With only a few exceptions, these behavior patterns are shared by all, but with differing degrees of participation. For example, some do not regularly engage in certain economic, religious, or social practices. This differential participation, in combination with physical criteria, defines certain statuses. One of these is that of Indian. This status is accorded low rank and, as far as behavior associated with status is assumed to be of aboriginal derivation, there is a blockage to social assimilation. Until completely random placement of the descendants of the two once distinct cultural groups occurs, cultural assimilation may be complete but social assimilation is not.

NOTES

1. The accompanying report by Thomas B. Hinton, covering an ethnographic survey of northern and eastern Sonora, should remedy the present lack of ethnographic information for this region.

2. This population figure for the Opatas and Jovas has been questioned. Some feel that a more likely figure would be 30,000.

3. This is a variant spelling of a term often rendered "Aibine." The Aibine appear to have been a group of Opatas who occupied the Mátape valley.

4. Literally, in Spanish, the ancestors or the predecessors. As used in Marobavi, however, *antepasados* refers primarily to the indigenous people, now gone, who once inhabited the area. It comes to have the same meaning as Indian or *indígena,* but with reference to past time.

5. A random sample of the sherd material found on the terrace was made and a few stone artifacts were collected in the village. This collection is in the Arizona State Museum, University of Arizona, Tucson.

6. This house type is found throughout the San Miguel valley and in most of Sonora to the east (Hinton 1956b).

7. All these data were collected by the author. All but half a dozen ages were collected either from the individuals involved or from immediate relatives. Due to the absence of accurate birth records the possibility of error is great. Stated ages were often checked with contemporaries of the individual involved. One old woman who gave her age as "about 60" was remembered as an adult during the childhood of other villagers who now are over 60; her age was finally estimated to be 79. Some women deducted several years from their age as given by brothers and friends; their ages were amended.

8. There is a discussion in Taylor, 1933 of bracero attitudes toward the United States, as well as of their reaction to and their position in their own village when they return from the United States. The attitudes described by Taylor closely parallel those found in Marobavi.

9. For a more extensive treatment of the geography of a similar area see Hewes, 1935. This short article has a good description of the sugar cane-corn-beans-wheat agriculture as it was in the 1930's. The report deals with Huépac, a town in the Sonora River valley.

10. For a description of how these foods are made see Hinton, 1956a.

11. The manufacturing techniques used in the production of this pottery are described in Owen, 1957.

12. The term "married" is herein used to refer to those couples who more or less permanently reside together. It includes people who are legally married and those who are not and is consistent with the usage of the term in Marobavi.

13. The Spanish terms are, respectively: *huero, rubio, blanco, moreno, prieto,* and *negro.*

14. Both this system of classification and that dealing with wealth position were derived from conversations with inhabitants. Lists were made of those people considered to be Indian and White, while "mixed" is a compilation of people so indicated by informants and a residual category consisting of households not classified by the villagers.

TABLE 1. DISTRIBUTION BY AGE AND SEX OF THE POPULATION OF MAROBAVI AS OF JUNE, 1955*

Age Group	Male	Female	Total
0- 5	32	27	59
6-10	24	19	43
11-15	17	18	35
16-20	17	17	34
21-25	10	12	22
26-30	8	11	19
31-35	12	9	21
36-40	6	8	14
41-45	11	7	18
46-50	2	4	6
51-55	5	5	10
56-60	5	3	8
61-65	4	3	7
66-70	2	5	7
71-75	2	3	5
76-80	2	2	4
81-85	0	0	0
Total	159	153	312

*The form 0-5 has been used instead of the more customary 0-4 because of the figuring of the child's age, in the village, at one year at the date of birth (Foster 1948: 28).

TABLE 3. COMPOSITION OF HOUSEHOLDS IN MAROBAVI

Composition	Number of		
	Households	Adults*	Children
1. Married couple with children . . .	27	78	96
2. Married couple with children and parent of husband	1	4	1
3. Married couple with children and parent of wife . .	5	19	19
4. Widower(er) with children	6	17	8
5. Married couple alone	2	4	0
6. Single woman with children	4	10	10
7. Single woman with grandchildren . . .	2	9	7
8. Single woman with children and woman's parent(s)	2	6	4
9. Non-married relatives	4	12	2
10. Men living alone . .	2	2	0
11. Women living alone .	4	4	0
Total	59	165	147

*Over sixteen years of age

TABLE 2 FREQUENCY OF SURNAMES IN MAROBAVI

Names	No. of household heads bearing name	No. of individuals bearing name
1. Acuna	0	1
2. Andrade	4	28
3. Angulo	1	4
4. Anzar	1	2
5. Brockman	2	15
6. Carillo	1	1
7. Carranza	1	5
8. Castillo	1	3
9. Contreras	0	5
10. Coronado	0	3
11. Cruz	0	10
12. Encinas	0	2
13. Enrique	0	7
14. Esquer	1	3
15. Fernandez	4	22
16. Guaraqui*	5	22
17. Lopez	3	33
18. Martinez	10	53
19. Matta	1	8
20. Mendoza	3	16
21. Miranda	1	1
22. Moreno	0	1
23. Nunez	1	6
24. Olivarilla	0	1
25. Paco	1	1
26. Paredes	1	4
27. Parra	1	1
28. Quintana	1	3
29. Quintanar	2	6
30. Ramirez	1	4
31. Ribas	0	3
32. Robles	1	3
33. Rodriguez	0	2
34. Roma	1	1
35. Santa Maria . . .	3	13
36. Savalsa	1	3
37. Sinohui*	2	3
38. Teran	1	1
39. Tomogua*	1	1
40. Trujillo	0	1
41. Valenzuela . . .	2	8
42. Vasquez	0	2

Married women and widows both have been classified by their maiden names.

*These names are considered to be aboriginal in origin by the villagers.

Table 4. Assignment of Households to Racial Category Contrasted With Economic Position

Economic Level	Racial Category		
	White	Mixed	Indian
Rich	3	0	0
Well-to-do	10	0	1
"Get-along"	11	15	9
Poor	0	2	8
Total	24	17	18

Table 5. Households Classified As To Physical Type Contrasted With Selected Criteria

Criteria	Physical Type					
	White %	(24) No.	Mixed %	(17) No.	Indian %	(18) No.
1. Farming own land or own more than 3 head of cattle	70.8	17	52.9	9	44.4	8
2. Make or sell *mescal*	12.5	3*	17.6	3	66.7	12
3. Household head born in Marobavi	50.0	12	76.5	13	94.4	17
4. One or more parents of household head born in Marobavi	54.2	13	76.5	13	88.9	16
5. Fatherless household	4.2	1	17.6	3	33.3	6
6. Reside in *casas de dos naves*	4.2	1	64.7	11	66.7	12
7. Have worked in the United States	37.5	9	35.3	6	11.1	2

*All three households sell *mescal*, none makes it.

TABLE 6

CEREMONIAL CALENDAR OF MAROBAVI

Date	Holiday	Observances
January 6	Epiphany	Two or more days of dancing by *pastores*.
LENT		Prayer services every Friday night.
	Ash Wednesday	Nothing.
	San Jose Day	Prayers in church in the morning.
	Palm Sunday	Prayers in church in the morning.
	Holy Thursday	Prayers in church in the morning; church bells substituted for by drum and *matraca;* altar draped in black; afternoon procession; *fariseos* appear at night; procession at night.
	Good Friday	*Fariseos* active all day; noon procession—sentencing of Christ; procession in later afternoon; procession at night; *farieseo* activity reaches peak.
	Holy Saturday	Figure of Judas taken from house to house by *fariseos* collecting food and money; *fariseos* are whipped by *angelitos* while Judas is burned outside the church—women pray inside. End of "sadness" of Lent; drinking and dancing begin.
	Easter Sunday	Procession in morning; baptism of *fariseos; taguaro* held in later afternoon. Social dance in evening that may last two or more days.
May	Month of the Virgin	Prayers in church every night.
May 3	Day of the Holy Cross	Procession to a nearby hill; new house crosses made.
May 15	San Isidro Labrador	Patron of the village—mass; procession with image to fields; four day fiesta, 13th to 16th, social dancing in plaza under a dance ramada called the *parian*.
June	Month of the Sacred Heart	Prayer services every night.
June 6	San Antonio	Prayer services in the morning.
June 24	San Juan	Procession with image to river at night; bathing of image and the hair of participants; expectancy of onset of rainy season.
October 4	San Francisco	Those who are able travel to fiesta at Magdalena (Dobyns 1950).
December 24	Christmas Eve	Said to be the third most important fiesta after Lent and San Isidro's.

Fig. 1. LOOKING EAST ACROSS THE RIO CANON VALLEY.

Fig. 2. THE MAIN PLAZA OF THE VILLAGE.

FIG. 3. A SINGLE ROOM HOUSE WITH COOKING RAMADA.

FIG. 4. THE SCHOOL.

FIG. 5. STREET SCENE. A *CASA DE DOS NAVES*.

FIG. 6. A MUCH TRAVELED INDIVIDUAL.

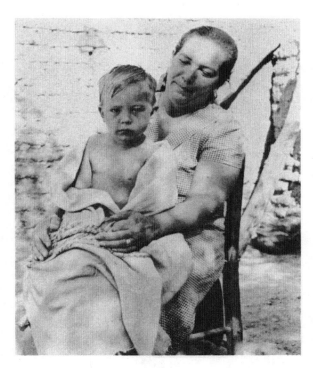

FIG. 7. A FAMILY CLASSIFIED AS WHITE.

FIG. 8. BASEBALL TEAM OF MEN FROM ALL STATUS GROUPS.

Fig. 9. A FAMILY CONSIDERED TO BE INDIAN.

FIG. 10. THE WEALTHIEST MAN IN THE VILLAGE.

FIG. 11. THRESHING WHEAT IN THE RIVER BOTTOM.

FIG.12. THE ONLY MAN SUPPORTED SOLELY BY CATTLE RAISING.

FIG. 13. A *MESCAL* STILL IN OPERATION.

Fig. 14. THE LARGEST STORE IN THE VILLAGE.

Fig. 15. THE CHURCH.

FIG. 16. BOY AND GIRL WEARING *HABITOS*.

FIG. 17. BEFORE A PROCESSION.

FIG. 18. THE CEMETERY.

REFERENCES

BANNON, J. F.
  1955   The Mission Frontier in Sonora, 1620-1687. *United States Catholic Historical Society, Monograph Series,* 26. New York.

BARTLETT, J. R.
  1854   *Personal Narrative of Explorations and Incidents in Texas, New Mexico, California, Sonora and Chihuahua.* 2 vols. D. Appleton and Company, New York.

BEALS, RALPH
  1932   The Comparative Ethnology of Northern Mexico before 1750. *Ibero-Americana:* 2. University of California Press, Berkeley.
  1943   The Aboriginal Culture of the Cahita Indians. *Ibero-Americana:* 19. University of California Press, Berkeley.

BOLTON, HERBERT, (EDITOR AND TRANSLATOR)
  1948   *Kino's Historical Memoir of Pimería Alta.* University of California Press, Berkeley.

CENSO DIVISION TERRITORIAL DEL ESTADO DE SONORA
  1901   Oficina Tipográfica de la Secretaria de Fomento, Mexico.

COUES, ELLIOT (EDITOR)
  1895   *The Expeditions of Zebulon Montgomery Pike, to Headwaters of the Mississippi River, through Louisiana Territory, and in New Spain, during the Years 1805-6-7.* 3 vols. (Reprinted from the original of 1810). Frances P. Harper, New York.

CUENTA DEL ERARIO DEL ESTADO DE SONORA
  1894   *Correspondiente al Año de 1893.* Imprenta de E. Gaxiola y Compañia, Guaymas.

DOBYNS, H. F. (EDITOR)
  1950   The Fiesta of St. Francis Xaxier: Magdalena, Sonora, Mexico. *Kiva,* Vol. 16, Nos. 1 and 2, pp. 1-32. Tucson.

EZELL, PAUL
  1955   The Hispanic Acculturation of the Gila River Pimas. MS, doctoral dissertation, The University of Arizona, Tucson.

FOSTER, G. M.
  1948   Empire's Children: The People of Tzintzuntzan. *Institute of Social Anthropology, Publication* 6. Smithsonian Institution, Washington.

GUITERAS, EUSEBIO (TRANSLATOR)
  1951   *Rudo Ensayo, by an unknown Jesuit Padre, 1763.* Arizona Silhouettes, Tucson.

HAMMOND, GEORGE AND AGAPITO REY (EDITORS)
  1928   *Obregón's History of 16th Century Explorations in Western America.* Wetzel Publishing Company, Los Angeles.

HARDY, R. W. H.

1829   *Travels in the Interior of Mexico in 1825-1828.* H. Colburn and R. Bentley, London.

HEWES, LESLIE

1935   Huépac: An Agricultural Village of Sonora, Mexico. *Economic Geography,* Vol. 11, No. 3, pp. 284-292. Worcester.

HINTON, THOMAS

1956a   A Description of the Contemporary Use of an Aboriginal Sonoran Food. *Kiva,* Vol. 21, Nos. 3 and 4, pp. 27-28. Tucson.

1956b   Personal Communication.

1959   A Survey of Indian Assimilation in Eastern Sonora. *Anthropological Papers of The University of Arizona,* No. 4. Tucson.

HRDLICKA, ALES

1904   Notes on the Indians of Sonora, Mexico. *American Anthropologist,* Vol. 6, No. 1, pp. 51-89. Menasha.

JOHNSON, J. B.

1950   The Opata, an Inland Tribe of Sonora. *University of New Mexico Publications in Anthropology,* No. 6. University of New Mexico Press, Albuquerque.

LUMHOLTZ, CARL

1912   *New Trails in Mexico.* Charles Scribners' Sons, New York.

MINTZ, SIDNEY AND ERIC WOLF

1950   An Analysis of Ritual Co-Parenthood (Compadrazgo). *Southwestern Journal of Anthropology,* Vol. 6, No. 4, pp. 341-368. Albuquerque.

NYE, W. F. (TRANSLATOR)

1861   *Sonora: Its Extent, Populations, Natural Productions, Indian Tribes, Mineral Lands.* Translated from the Spanish of Francisco Velasco. H. H. Bancroft and Company, San Francisco.

OWEN, ROGER

1957   Paddle and Anvil Appearance of Some Sonoran Pottery. *American Antiquity,* Vol. 22, No. 3, p. 291. Salt Lake City.

1958   Easter Ceremonies Among Opata Descendants of Northern Sonora, Mexico. *Kiva,* Vol. 23, No. 4, pp. 1-11. Tucson.

REDFIELD, ROBERT, RALPH LINTON AND MELVILLE HERSKOVITS

1936   Memorandum for the Study of Acculturation. *American Anthropologist,* Vol. 38, No. 1, pp. 149-152. Menasha.

RESUMENES DEL CENSO DEL ESTADO DE SONORA

1895   Imprenta y Encuadernación de Eduardo Gaxiola, Guaymas.

SAUER, CARL
1932   The Road to Cíbola. *Ibero-Americana:* 3. University of California Press, Berkeley.
1934   The Distribution of Aboriginal Tribes and Languages in Northwestern Mexico. *Ibero-Americana:* 5. University of California Press, Berkeley.
1935   Aboriginal Populations of Northwestern Mexico. *Ibero-Americana:* 10. University of California Press, Berkeley.

SERVICE, E. R., AND H. S.
1954   *Tobatí: Paraguayan Town.* University of Chicago Press, Chicago.

SMITH, BUCKINGHAM (TRANSLATOR)
1929   *Relation of Alvar Nuñez Cabeza de Vaca.* Grabhorn Press, San Francisco.

SOCIAL SCIENCE RESEARCH COUNCIL
1954   Acculturation: An Exploratory Formulation. *American Anthropologist,* Vol. 56, No. 6, pp. 973-1002. Menasha.

SPICER, E. H.
1954a   Potam: A Yaqui Village in Sonora. *Memoirs of the American Anthropological Association,* No. 77. Menasha.
1954b   Spanish-Indian Acculturation in the Southwest. *American Anthropologist,* Vol. 56, No. 4, pp. 663-684. Menasha.

TAYLOR, PAUL
1933   A Spanish-Mexican Peasant Community: Arandas in Jalisco, Mexico. *Ibero-Americana:* 4. University of California Press, Berkeley.

TREUTLEIN, THEODORE (EDITOR AND TRANSLATOR)
1949   Sonora, A Description of the Province, by Ignaz Pfefferkorn. *Coronado Cuarto Centennial Publications,* Vol. 12. University of New Mexico Press, Albuquerque.

VILLA, EDUARDO
1951   *Historia del Estado de Sonora.* Segunda Edición. Editorial Sonora, Hermosillo.

WHETTEN, NATHAN
1948   *Rural Mexico.* University of Chicago Press, Chicago.
1950   The Rise of a Middle Class in Mexico. *Publicaciones de la Oficina de Ciencias Sociales,* No. 2. Union Panamericana, Washington.

WYLLYS, RUFUS
1932   The French in Sonora (1850-1854). *University of California Publications in History,* Vol. 21. University of California Press, Berkeley.